Interviewing Skills for Legal Professionals

DOUG COCHRAN

2004
EMOND MONTGOMERY PUBLICATIONS LIMITED
TORONTO, CANADA

Printed in Canada.

Edited, designed, and typeset by WordsWorth Communications, Toronto.
Cover design by Susan Darrach, Darrach Design.

We acknowledge the financial support of the Government of Canada through the Book Publishing Industry Development Program (BPIDP) for our publishing activities.

The events and characters depicted in this book are fictitious. Any similarity to actual persons, living or dead, is purely coincidental.

National Library of Canada Cataloguing in Publication

Cochran, Doug, 1950-
    Interviewing skills for legal professionals / Doug Cochran.

Includes index.
ISBN 978-1-55239-102-0

    1. Interviewing in law practice—Canada.   2. Attorney and client.   3. Investigations.   I. Title.

KE346.C65 2003   340'.023'71   C2003-907396-3
KF311.C628 2003

Dedication

I have taught legal interviewing skills for 14 years, during which time I worked with UBC Law School students in an interviewing competition. These experiences have offered me tremendous opportunity for developing and testing my thoughts about the legal interviewing process and how best to encourage the skills of students in this area. Therefore, I would like to express my thanks particularly to all the students with whom I have had the pleasure of working. I am indebted to them for their commitment to learning this art and for their perceptiveness in analyzing and critiquing legal interviews.

— Doug Cochran

Table of Contents

INTRODUCTION
Client-Centred Interviewing

The focus of this text is on client-centred interviewing. Since legal clients are not assembly line products with identical issues, needs, and emotions, each must be approached as a unique individual. The needs of each client must be assessed and matched to the range of options that the law firm has available to it. Client-centred interviewing implies that it is more important that the client be comfortable with the interview process than the paralegal or lawyer. At the same time, this approach has developed from the recognition that effective representation of clients is rooted in a good working relationship with each client. Each client's needs must be assessed and her tolerance for the range of options that a law firm has in representing her interests must be considered.

The law firm that blindly forges ahead and represents the client without taking care to accommodate her particular personality and physical, economic, or emotional needs will end up with a less-satisfied client, and perhaps without a client at all. Law firms rarely lure clients with half-price sales, promotional give-aways, or air miles points, so what a law firm has to offer that sets it above others is the quality of its service. Any practitioner who suggests that simply giving good representation will universally result in satisfied clients hasn't been paying attention. Time and again I have seen lawyers provide excellent representation for a client but leave the client ill-informed, confused, and even angry at the lawyer before the process is concluded. I have to admit that I have taken advantage of an opponent's dissatisfaction with their counsel to extract a benefit for my client, because if the opponent is dissatisfied, she won't trust her legal counsel. This distrust gives your client a distinct advantage.

In adopting a client-centred approach to interviewing, I believe a client who is actively involved in problem solving with the law firm, who is kept informed at all stages in the process, and whose emotional inhibitors are recognized and addressed will be more satisfied and better served over the long run. Occasionally, it is necessary to sacrifice what we see as efficiency to ensure that the client receives the best representation in resolving their problem. I firmly believe that, over the course of representing a client in solving their legal concern, a client-centred approach will dramatically reduce the cost to the client and result in greater satisfaction with the legal representation the firm provides.

The client and the law firm are partners in a very demanding process. I think of it like climbing a rock face, roped together with other climbers. You would probably not want to undertake this task if you felt one of the climbers was emotionally unstable. Persons involved in litigation have a strong tendency toward emotional instability. Ignoring indicators or emotional concerns, hoping they will just miraculously disappear, is about as effective as wishing the boogie man away. It only works if you are *not* in a slasher movie and the danger is only in your imagination. With legal issues, the danger is real.

Law firms are not set up to provide therapy, and I would never suggest that this is a role paralegals should take on. But being aware of, acknowledging, and addressing a client's emotional concerns is necessary in order for the client to participate in the process in a manner that helps the law firm do its job effectively.

What this book tries to do is provide a work-study opportunity for students of legal interviewing. It is written from the perspective of the paralegal, since I have had considerable experience teaching legal interviewing to paralegal students and there is little material available for this purpose. I have tried to declare my biases with regard to the process of legal interviewing and, at the same time, give students the benefit of various perspectives that I have been exposed to over the years.

Legal interviewing is a process that can be

> **A** client in a divorce matter would break into tears every time she came into my office. It is, of course, not unusual for a client to cry in the process of divorce proceedings, but what was unusual is that this client cried *every* time. On one occasion, we almost made it to the end of an interview without the shedding of tears, but when we dealt with a problem involving one of her children she began to cry. She said, "Oh, damn, I promised myself I would get through it this time without crying." I think both of us had been looking for a breakthrough where she could discuss the divorce without sobbing. This was a mature, intelligent, and caring individual. She had a therapist whom she was seeing for the emotional fallout from the divorce. Nevertheless, she had so much emotion invested in the legal proceedings that she needed an outlet within that process. For each interview we did, it took longer than usual to get beyond her emotions and deal with the matters necessary to the process, but if I had ignored the emotional component, it would still be there, unacknowledged, and it would ultimately impede the process and potentially sabotage any resolution to the legal concerns.

"Being aware of, acknowledging, and addressing a client's emotional concerns is necessary for the client to participate in the process in a manner that helps the law firm do its job effectively."

learned and dramatic improvement can be achieved by almost everyone who directs their attention to the task. I often tell competitors in a law school competition that I coach that when it comes to interviewing I can make a silk purse out of a sow's ear. While the comment is meant to be humorous, the point is real: students who earnestly focus on learning this craft can achieve a great transformation in the process.

Good legal interviewing has the capacity to access information that would otherwise remain undetected, in such a way that the client is involved, feels supported, and is supportive of the process.

Bad legal interviewing leaves serious gaps in information. The insensitivity of the interviewer can alienate the client, leaving her feeling unsupported and less able or inclined to participate in the discovery process. As an interviewer you have the power to choose the approach that best suits your needs and will result in the most positive outcome.

INTRODUCTION QUESTIONS

1. What is client-centred interviewing?

2. Outline two consequences of good legal interviewing and two of bad legal interviewing.

INTRODUCTION EXERCISES

Watch some interviews on television or listen to some on the radio. Consider the orientation of the interviewer.

1. Does she have an agenda of her own in conducting the interview?

2. Is she concerned that the interviewee be made to feel comfortable, in control, open in making his comments?

3. What is the consequence of the interviewer's style?

4. How might you conduct the interview differently, if it was in the context of legal fact finding?

CHAPTER 1

What's Behind Good Client Interviewing?

In Brief

This chapter discusses your role during the law firm's assistance to a client through the various stages of its representation of her. You are encouraged to consider what motivates a client and how obstacles to communication undermine effective client representation.

CONTINUUM

The process is really a continuum of actions, from the initial client contact through to closing the file. Although the lawyer can but *should not* be involved in every stage, you, as a legal professional, can, and often should, be involved in all phases, from the birth of the file to when it is sent to storage. This may sound strange. After all, the lawyer is the brains, the nerve centre of the legal action. Logically, he must be involved from beginning to end.

However, there are two problems with this thinking: the first is the assumption that the lawyer is the key person in the process. As you will see in the material dealing with client-centred interviewing, the client is the focal point in any legal action. All the efforts of the law firm must radiate from the needs and comfort of the client and keep her as the centre of its efforts. The potential error is in thinking that the lawyer needs to be involved in all stages of the process.

The second erroneous assumption is that the best way of serving the client is for the lawyer to "have his nose in everything" that goes on in dealing with the client. Certainly, each lawyer has his or her level of comfort with delegating responsibility. However, with well-trained professionals, lawyers will not only be comfortable but will come to *rely* on their staff to complete tasks in a competent and independent manner. As a professional, the better you are at these tasks, the more valuable you are to the firm. The more valuable you are, the more potential you have to command the two Rs: respect and remuneration. Frankly, employers of legal professionals reward excellence. A law office, more than most environments, profits from quality in work, and those profits mean more money available to reward valued staff.

What follows now is the sequence of (three) stages in a legal proceeding. Each stage includes commentary about how your work can facilitate and reinforce the work done by lawyers in the firm. Appendix A provides abbreviated commentary about these tasks.

INITIAL CLIENT CONTACT

Here, you face two elements: building rapport with the client and assisting with identification of the issues confronting the client. As we will discuss in some detail throughout the text, a client's comfort level with the law firm usually determines the degree to which she shares information with you.

> "Most people do not require a lifelong commitment before they share intimate details of their lives, but they do require trust."

Most people do not require a lifelong commitment before they share intimate details of their lives, but they do require trust. People need to feel assured that you will not use their secrets, fears, and vulnerable experiences in a way that will harm them. Clients want the security of knowing that you will only use this information to help them. This only makes sense: why else would a law firm representing a client want information if it was not to help the client? This, of course, is a rational perspective. However, people who need legal advice are usually feeling "beat up" in one way or another. The beat-up feeling might be physical, emotional—often financial—but it is frequently there. From this beat-up perspective, the world is a less predictable place, perhaps even a scary place.

The development of rapport with a client is important to the firm's long-term relationship with the client. Empathy and understanding can help in obtaining information necessary to assist the client with her concerns. This rapport or comfortable relationship may not play a role in any particular interview, but it may prove to be crucial at another time in another circumstance. Think of it as having a Mars bar in your coat pocket—sometimes a comforting thought, useful if you miss a meal, and downright essential if you get caught in a snowdrift in your car.

After a particularly traumatic experience, when a client has been harmed in a

A few years ago, I was on holiday in the Gulf Islands. In an idle moment I ran my hand through my hair and noticed some fairly substantial bumps on my scalp—and these were pretty big! Three of them were the size of a nickel and stood up from my scalp about the width of my finger. In shock, I concluded that I had brain cancer. I imagined the wildly multiplying cancer cells bursting through my cranium, distorting my scalp with these large lumps. With a certain panic, I tried to prepare myself for the end. The biggest problem was that I was days away from obtaining any medical advice. Later, when I saw my doctor, it took him about five minutes to diagnose the problem as seborrhea, a scalp condition. He prescribed a dandruff shampoo. While this was a bit anti-climactic—no tearful goodbyes, no 21-gun salute—it was a welcome relief. My point? Even the smartest people, given limited information and dealing with events outside their expertise, can come to the wrong conclusions.

physical, emotional, or financial way, you could be the first person that the client will find herself trusting. Or maybe not. It is really up to you to become that trusted person, to facilitate the sharing of information. Your efforts to get through the client's defences may not always work, but not to try to do so is a failure on your part.

The trust you establish with the client helps her to speak freely. In this way, you gather information that will be essential in helping the lawyer identify the issues. Although clients, when they come to see the lawyer, often have a clear idea of what needs to be resolved, they may also have misdiagnosed their situation. With complete information the lawyer can correctly analyze the issues and chart a reasonable course for resolving the conflict.

In the process of fact gathering, not all "facts" are equal. Some facts are more compelling—the busload of nuns who observe the incident from beginning to end— while others are less helpful—Arty, the local heroin addict/drug dealer, who can vouch for your client's whereabouts. The process of gathering information includes the assessment of the value of that information and looking to secondary sources that confirm or undermine that information. Uncertainty or loose ends are unacceptable in a law office if anything can be done to eliminate them. Your job is akin to a bloodhound's, relentlessly pursuing leads in order to secure information that will help the lawyer advise the client. The effectiveness of this process can make the difference between winning or losing the client's case.

Legal/Non-Legal Issues

Counsel (lawyers) sometimes choose to ignore anything that isn't narrowly defined as a "legal problem" because these matters are confusing or emotionally troubling. Some lawyers describe these issues as "touchy-feely."

From the opposite perspective, a lawyer who takes a "client-centred" approach will insist that unless the non-legal aspects of the client's circumstance are addressed they will continually interfere with resolving the client's difficulties. While I largely agree with the latter approach, I disagree generally with the legal/non-legal dichotomy. Anything that interferes with a person's ability to deal effectively with legal issues is a problem.

Rather than getting caught up in semantics, we should try to clear away—or at least minimize—any obstacle to client communication and action.

Frequently, the expression "the lawyer advises, the client instructs" is used to characterize the unique relationship between lawyer and client. This axiom reminds us of the limit on the lawyer's control or authority in dealing with the client's concerns. In my opinion, lawyers cannot be reminded of this important principle too often. Although they rightly exert a powerful influence over clients, many lawyers tend to forget who is directing the show.

> **"Anything that interferes with a person's ability to deal effectively with legal issues is a problem."**

How then can lawyers advise clients if they do not know the factors that are influencing a client's decision making? Some lawyers believe in the "hands off" approach and avoid exploring the "personal" factors that drive the client to act in the way that she does. The lawyer's advice, now limited to his understanding of the narrow legal issue, may have disastrous consequences for the client. Perhaps lawyers cannot be blamed if the client takes his advice and blindly applies it without playing out the consequences. Blameless as the lawyer may be, why not help the client to think things through and to understand the consequences of her actions on her life outside the litigation? We are a service industry after all.

I would like you to prepare a new will for me.

All right. Have you considered what changes to your old will you wish to make?

I want to cut my son entirely out of my will.

All right. Any other changes?

No, that's it.

OK. We'll have that ready by Friday.

One perspective on this exchange is that it is not the law firm's business if the client wishes to take such an extreme step. I don't agree. There are aspects of legal advice here that a lawyer should go into, and a good interviewer can help the client sort through her feelings on this matter.

Why do you want to cut your son out of your will?

He's just wild and unpredictable. He's probably into drugs and he refuses to make anything of his life.

How old is your son?

Nineteen.

And do you think that his lifestyle is not likely to change?

Well … maybe … probably given some time … I mean, I was pretty wild in my youth, gave my parents some things to worry about, but I just hate what this is doing to his father.

Have you spoken to your husband about cutting your son out of your will?

Well, no … I guess maybe that might be wise … at least a first step.

Shall we wait to hear back from you?

Yes, please … let's keep this on hold for a while … until I've worked it through.

There is a balance between respecting the client's right to make her decision (and following through with her instructions) and helping the client to sort out exactly what she wants to accomplish. The law firm should not and cannot tell the client, *I wouldn't do that if I were you,* but it is legitimate—and indeed may be of great assistance to the client—to point out aspects that she may not have considered. This may cause the client to rethink her instructions; at the very least, the client will be acting in a reasoned manner and is more likely to make a decision that she will be happy with in the future. In the example above, the results may avoid costly estate litigation.

To Act or Not To Act

Few people like to waste time, even fewer, money. Once the issues have been identified by the lawyer, a certain clarity usually emerges.

The lawyer's analysis, based on the information elicited from the client, must include alternative actions (or non-action) by the client. The client has the right to hear from the lawyer what the likely outcomes would be from each course of action and to have some assistance from counsel in choosing the most appropriate course of action at any given time.

New facts (acquiring information either favourable or unfavourable to the client's case) or changes in the law can all affect whether a particular course of action or non-action is appropriate. The client might then decide that there is not enough information to pursue an action at this time. However, six months later, when the "smoking gun" is uncovered, the decision might be to move ahead with an action. Continuing to assist in preparing the file, including maintaining and building rapport with the client and conducting effective interviews with other sources that come to light, will prove invaluable in representing her interests.

NEGOTIATION AND TRIAL PREPARATION

In the process of negotiating a settlement of an action, it is vitally important that both the client and the opponent are convinced that their law firms are well prepared for trial. Cases aren't settled out of court because that is "the right thing to do"; they are settled because each side is convinced that they could do worse at trial, and both sides want to move on with their lives. A large part of this process is getting the other side to see how effective your firm will be in presenting your client's case in court. For example, if the other side can visualize your client's *winning case*, then they will be prepared to settle in a manner that is advantageous to your client.

Your interviews with the client will help prepare her for the discovery process and will help shape the lawyer's strategy in directing the action. Be receptive to new information "popping up" as the litigation proceeds, and be alert that information that either was not or did not appear relevant at one stage in the proceedings may become crucial at a later stage. The discovery process, which varies among jurisdictions, is the means used by each law firm to find out as much information, both positive and negative, about the other side's case.

The earlier your firm has sufficient facts to proceed to trial, the earlier serious negotiations can begin, and thus your client can grapple with the thorny settlement question of what is enough or what is too much. Negotiations and trial preparations continue simultaneously until a resolution has been reached, either through settlement or judicial pronouncement.

TRIAL AND POST-TRIAL PROCESSES

Even at the point of trial, legal professionals continue to play an important role in assisting counsel in representing clients. Most commonly, you would organize the lawyer's interview notes to facilitate his examination of witnesses.

Interviewing witnesses immediately prior to their testimony, to help prepare them for the trial, may be another role played by a paralegal. However, unless the lawyer practises on the British model (solicitors interview clients, barristers appear in court), most Canadian lawyers want to do the final preparation themselves.

One exception to this preferred method of operation is the emergency witness interview. Mid-trial, circumstances may dictate that a witness who did not initially appear to be necessary will have to be called to testify. The lawyer, who is busy in court all day, would then need to have the witness prepared on short notice.

Post-trial procedures are often delegated to paralegals. While lawyers often want to quickly move on to the next big file, maximizing their productive capacity, good client service involves tying up loose ends and ensuring that what the client achieved through your firm's representation is not diminished post-trial. By this time, you should have a good relationship with the client and have a complete understanding of the file. Therefore, taking care of the myriad details to conclude your firm's representation of the client may often fall onto your shoulders. If the client has been successful in her action, this can be a very rewarding time in representing her. If the client has been unsuccessful, the client will need to be supported in this transition.

Regardless of the outcome, effective representation of the client, even post-trial, is essential for her satisfaction and, of course, instrumental in whether she will use or recommend your firm's services in the future. Surprisingly, successful representation is not the ultimate determinant of whether a client recommends your services to others or even uses your firm to help them out of the next jam they find themselves in. Trust and good rapport matter more.

Appendix A lists the various stages of client representation, their purposes, and the interviewer's tasks at each stage.

SEEN THROUGH MY EYES

A legal dispute can be seen as a difference in perspectives between parties about the same incident(s) or set of facts. In some cases, there actually are good guys and bad guys: one party (who wishes to avoid being held legally responsible) is seen as liable for another person's misfortune; the other party in the dispute is the "victim." Usually, each party is acting more or less in good faith; they just happen to view the world, or at least this set of circumstances, differently. I say "more or less" in good faith. In my experience, few disputes include a completely innocent party; often, both people have, in their own way, helped fuel the conflict. However, in most cases, one person is most culpable.

Here is an example by way of a personal confession. In my student days I occupied a basement suite with my girlfriend. It was a nasty and brutish place, but we called it home. Our landlord was nice enough so long as there was no dispute between us, but when a dispute arose he became unyielding and unpleasant. Our basement suite developed some "water problems"—the part of the basement outside our kitchen door was a small lake, water lapped up under the floor boards, the shower backed up, and the toilet rarely flushed.

My girlfriend and I tried to be patient, but when the water problem did not get resolved, we told the landlord we were moving out at the end of the month. The landlord's response was to inform us that we were required by law to give one calendar month's notice. This meant that we would be paying rent for two places at once—something we couldn't afford. This was long before I went to law school, and our landlord seemed to know what he was talking about. I was quite intimidated by his self-assuredness.

I felt that one factor gave us some leverage: the suite was really not fit for habitation (unless one was a duck). To his credit, the landlord was trying to solve the water problem, and from time to time various people inspected or tried to fix the problem, although without doing any major digging.

So we had this legal dispute: the landlord insisted that we pay another month's rent, and we were refusing because of the flooding. Then, about ten days before we planned to leave, something strange happened. The water began to recede. One morning, the lake was considerably reduced in size. This created a conundrum: by this time, our relationship with this landlord was soured to the point where we did not want to live in his house. We had made other arrangements. Yet, the foundation of our "defence" was evaporating before our eyes.

What to do? What would any self-respecting litigant do? Quietly, we began pouring pots of water into the lake to stop it receding. Late at night and early in the morning we would sneak into the darkened basement and deposit enough water to bring the lake back up to a level that maintained our justification for vacating the premises. (We had moved by then.)

No matter how much I justified my actions, clearly I was not acting in an open and honest manner. This is the lot of litigants in our society, they tend to justify their actions by demonizing the opponent—and honesty becomes a relative term. This relativity, by the way, is something to keep in mind when interviewing clients about their legal concerns.

Without a legal process for resolving disputes, the two sides would be in a continual stalemate. The situation would be akin to the classic children's taunt:

> You're a liar/thief/bully (or whatever).

> Am not!

> Are too!!

> Am not!!

> Are too!!!

Adding exclamation marks brings the basic conflict no closer to resolution. Now, if you impose a system where somebody "bigger" (the courts/justice system) can impose a judgment, then the elements of a dispute resolution mechanism begin to be put in place.

An interesting aspect of such a process is the pressure on the parties to find their own resolution given the cost and uncertainty inherent in the legal process. Interestingly, because the court/justice system outcome is unpredictable, the parties to the dispute often prefer to resolve things themselves rather than leaving it to chance.

> We might as well compromise and reach a resolution; otherwise,
> who knows what crazy results the courts might come up with.

I have heard that when Richard Nixon was president of the United States and Henry Kissinger was the secretary of state, they actually developed a strategy for dealing with foreign powers where Kissinger would tell their representatives,

> You know Nixon is crazy, there's no telling what he will do. I may be able to keep him in line, but this is the best I can do. If you don't accept these terms I shudder to think what might happen!

This may raise moral issues, and the strategy smacks of brinkmanship, but whatever other faults Nixon had, he is largely regarded as having had a successful foreign policy, at least from the American perspective.

Many people enter the litigation process believing that their version of events is so right that they can't possibly lose. They think that all their lawyer has to do is put the facts before the court and they will win, hands down. I suspect that these clients imagine the court severely chastising their opponent for even challenging the correctness of their case.

Our court system is less dramatic than that and more flawed. Your client must be made aware that even good representation cannot always carry the day. A livable settlement is almost always preferable to the uncertainty and the emotional and monetary expense of a trial.

The exception to this negotiated-settlement rule is when your client's opponent is so economically powerful and unaccountable that they believe they have nothing to lose in a court battle. In these "elephant-and-mouse" battles, as frustrating as they are, if your client wishes any form of justice, it will only come from the courts and only after the most complex and expensive legal processes have been exhausted.

Here is one example. An insurance company, ignoring its duty to actually "insure" clients from damage caused to them in motor vehicle crashes—against all morality and principles of contractual obligation—determines that they will deny coverage because the injured person's car suffered only "minimal damage." This blanket position, which ignores any evidence of real injury, is designed to save the insurer money because the cost of litigation to enforce an insured's rights is prohibitive. In one such instance, I am sure the insurer spent in the neighbourhood of $100,000 defending a claim that could have been settled for less than $15,000. For the elephant, the individual claim is irrelevant; it is done to discourage other potential litigants—that is the "benefit" to the insurer.

However, not all people in a legal dispute resolve differences through litigation. Mediation—with its win–win cachet—is becoming more common and acceptable. It has one big benefit over litigation: the element of certainty. In a mediated resolution, each side knows what the result will be before agreeing to it. Litigation, on the other hand, has been described by experienced counsel as a "crap shoot" where often in spite of the merits of an individual's case or the thoroughness of her representation, it is not possible to know the results until the judge gives her verdict. After that, it will usually be prohibitively expensive to appeal a decision and it is not possible to offer additional arguments after a judge has ruled on the issue in dispute.

One other dispute resolution process needs acknowledgment: the "truth and reconciliation" process instituted by Nelson Mandela in South Africa at the end of the apartheid era. This process is based on traditional justice as practised in tribal governance. With the adversarial model so often practised in North America, winning is everything. Success is determined solely by defeating the adversary before the court. No thought is given to an ongoing relationship between the parties or to the overall good (or bad) done to society by the dispute resolution process. In the adversarial process, it is often more important for the litigants to hide the truth from the decision maker than it is to disclose all the facts. It is irrelevant how devastating the decision is to one of the parties. The assumption is that society's interests are best served by having a system of justice to deal with disputes in an impartial manner, and individual outcomes are not important in that scheme of things.

Under a truth and reconciliation model, the community becomes involved in resolving a dispute. The interrelationships between the individual disputants and the larger community are central to the process, as is the importance of coming to a resolution that will allow the parties to co-exist in the future. Under this process, and of central importance, is the search for truth, because only where the truth is revealed can the parties leave the past behind and move ahead with their lives. The concept of punishment or retribution is replaced by the concept of reconciliation— living with, as opposed to destroying, your foes.

Some Canadian Aboriginal communities use restorative-justice programs in both criminal and civil cases. Many judges have accepted, even imposed, healing or talking circles in their sentencing decisions.

My purpose in outlining the concept of truth and reconciliation is not to advocate for the adoption of such a process. But it is wise to be aware that there are other ways of approaching a problem. A healthy society is aware of and open to alternatives.

> **"Not all people in a legal dispute resolve differences through litigation."**

WHY A LAWYER?

In order to consider the role of the law office in the client's life, we must first consider why the client has come to see a lawyer. There are two basic types of clients. The first is a person who wants help in enforcing a right that she feels she has: a landlord trying to evict a tenant who has declined to pay the rent, a person who wishes to sponsor a parent for immigration purposes, or an individual who has purchased a car and the transmission has failed after a week. In all of these instances, the client feels that she has a right to something. She needs to know if she is right in that belief—*legally right*, that is. She also needs to know what it would cost her to get what is rightfully hers. As you will quickly discover in your law office, there is a big difference between having a right to something and being able to enforce that right economically. One of society's most significant challenges is to try to bring the process of enforcing one's rights in line with most people's ability to afford to obtain satisfaction from the legal system.

The second type of client that law firms represent are those who are resisting claims made against them. Examples include the corporation being sued for negligently manufacturing a child's toy; the environmental protester charged with criminal trespass; the homeowner being sued because a branch from his tree broke off in a storm, crushing her neighbour's beloved dog. Similar to those people who wish to

> **"One of society's most significant challenges is to try to bring the process of enforcing one's rights in line with most people's ability to afford to obtain satisfaction from the legal system."**

As duty counsel, I have represented people arrested by the police and detained until they can appear before a judge to determine whether they will be released, perhaps on bail. The police generally don't detain people unless they believe that they will go right back to committing crimes or are unlikely to appear in court. In conducting interviews with many individuals in the jail cells, before speaking on their behalf in court, a surprising number of these people lie about their criminal records. They either claim to have no record (extremely unlikely since the police have not released them) or a more minor record than they actually have, or that they have never failed to appear in court on a criminal charge. Well, of course, when I spoke with the prosecutor, he would invariably have a copy of the actual criminal record.

If you base your submissions on the information that the client gives you, then you are "blindsided," left fumbling for some justification that would permit her release. It is particularly embarrassing if you have not had an opportunity to speak with the prosecutor. (You watch the Crown attorney as he takes the printout and, with a flourish, allows the pages to tumble from his outstretched arms to the floor—all six pages of your client's criminal record, about which she had developed amnesia.) Aside from the embarrassment aspect, if the lawyer is forewarned, he might muster some arguments—no convictions in the past four years—that might prevail and get her released.

enforce a right, these clients also need to know what their legal responsibilities are and what it will cost to defend themselves from the claims against them.

What service the law firm gives either type of client will depend on an analysis of the consequences of either taking a certain action or declining to take that action. The latter may be the more cost-effective option, but in all instances, lawyers and other legal professionals should help the client make an informed decision, one that will reduce the risk of a bad outcome and maximize her chances for a good result.

How do you fit in, given the role of the law firm in providing legal advice and representation in dealing with the client's legal concerns? As we will discuss a number of times in the text, only lawyers can give legal advice or represent the client in court. What then is left to do? A multitude of things.

The practice of law is not like television's popular legal dramas, where issues are resolved in the space of an hour (minus the time for commercials). Good legal representation is 90 percent perspiration and only 10 percent inspiration. It is in the hard work of gathering information, thoroughly understanding the complexities and details of the client's situation, and properly preparing for settlement or litigation that legal professionals show their worth.

MOTIVATION

To understand some of the potential pitfalls in the interviewing process, it may be helpful to consider the client's underlying motivations that may be involved at different stages in the process.

It is particularly important to look at factors that may cause clients to behave in ways that are unpredictable and even, sometimes, in ways that are demonstrably contrary to their best interests. Certainly, clients do not consciously undermine their legal representation, but it does happen that the actions or omissions of a client can do considerable damage to your firm's representation of them. An understanding of these factors may help us to "save clients from themselves."

Many lawyers, in dispensing legal advice, have developed a preamble that essentially says, "Based on the facts as you have outlined them to me … ." What this really says is, "If you haven't lied to me, then I feel safe in stating the following."

This underscores the frequency with which clients either lie to their lawyers or colour their version of events so significantly that caution must be exercised in relying on what the client says.

Most people would acknowledge that a lawyer needs to have accurate information in order to provide effective advice. However, for a variety of reasons, your client may fail to disclose information that could be crucial to your firm's successful representation of her. On the basis of a brief initial interview, even a trained psychologist would be unable to pinpoint the exact reason why any particular individual might compromise her chances of success in litigation by misinforming her legal representative. It would be a monumental task to illustrate all the possible traps used by your own clients. What we can do here is try to understand some of the underlying motivational factors that can lead a client to provide misleading information or withhold valuable information in an interview setting.

By understanding some of these motivational "glitches," your interviews can be structured to minimize the likelihood of these factors coming into play. By being alert to the potential for these corrupting influences, you will, hopefully, recognize when they are present, so you can take steps to overcome them.

To get beyond this "nasty business" of clients who mislead counsel, we must do everything we can to encourage candour from clients during the interview process. To decide what will work effectively, some analysis of the common reasons for client misrepresentation may assist. Appendix B presents a summary of obstacles to communication and some tactics to overcome them.

Like Me, Please Like Me

As already indicated, clients will often "screen out" facts that would place them in a negative light. The most obvious explanation for this is their need for you to like them. As any lawyer will tell you, you don't have to like a client to do a good job for her. Indeed, in some instances, liking a client can make you less objective.

In criminal matters, clients will often insist on their innocence. Yet, when the prosecution divulges the details of their case against your client, the inescapable reality of her guilt is obvious. Nevertheless, the client often wants her lawyer to believe in her innocence, thinking that her lawyer will only work hard and do a good job for an innocent client. This is not correct, of course. If lawyers worked only for innocent clients, very few accused persons would have good legal representation. Part of the challenge facing good criminal lawyers is obtaining an acquittal in circumstances where their client is, in fact, guilty.

> **"It is in the hard work of gathering information, thoroughly understanding the complexities and details of the client's situation, and properly preparing for settlement or litigation that legal professionals show their worth."**

> **"Certainly, clients do not consciously undermine their legal representation, but it does happen that the actions or omissions of a client can do considerable damage to your firm's representation of them."**

> **"One problem with misinformation is that the lawyer can't make an effective case as long as the client clings to the falsehood."**

In many areas of law, clients appear to feel that the law firm is more likely to do a good job if they are representing "the good guy." In family situations, clients will deny committing petty and vindictive acts, even to the point of being faced with indisputable proof. In a personal injury matter I dealt with some time back, my client insisted he had not run a red light, although every witness to whom I spoke confirmed that he had. Ultimately, it took the statement from his front-seat passenger to break down his resistance and admit the obvious.

One problem with misinformation is that the lawyer can't make an effective case as long as the client clings to the falsehood. Few situations exist where a lawyer can't improve the client's circumstances based on the true facts being revealed. However, in most instances, the client can do irreparable harm by misdirecting the lawyer.

Most clients don't tell outright lies, but many shade the truth. During your client interviews, you should be alert to a client's tendency to shave off negative information.

> **"Your relationship with the client must be established on the basis of trust and openness."**

How fast were you going?

How many drinks did you have that night?

How long did it take you to respond to the calls for help?

What time did you get home last night?

One potential way of dealing with this phenomenon is to "add back"—to assume exaggerations, based on your assumptions about how much "shaving" had been done by the witness. There are two concerns here. First, it adds another layer of dishonesty to your relationship with the client—and your client feels she has gotten away with her "white lie," when in fact you haven't accepted this information at face value. By doing this, you are taking an oppositional stance in relation to your client, which is clearly not your role in representing her. In its worst form, the client realizes your tendency to "discount" what she tells you, and she therefore feels compelled to "inflate" the story further, to compensate for the discounting.

The second problem is that you have reinforced her opinion that it is OK to mislead the law firm. In this scenario, the client concludes that you are "turning a blind eye" to the misstatement, that you are not concerned with the truth where it may harm her case. She believes that the two of you are engaged in a conspiracy in the fact finding.

Your relationship with the client must be established on the basis of trust and openness. If you allow a double standard to exist, you acquiesce in the client's actions, undermining these cornerstones of your relationship. How is the client to know when you really want her to be truthful and when you are looking for some discrete modification of the facts?

Control Freak

Some people need to control every situation they are in. One sign of this is the client carefully offering you snippets of information. These little packages are provided on what the client perceives as a *need-to-know* basis. In other words, the client insists on determining what is important for the law firm to know and what is best left unstated, perhaps never to be revealed. In this case, the law firm acts with tunnel vision on the issues.

This is not only discomforting but dangerous: the lawyer will not see the Mack truck until the fatal collision is imminent. Behaviour like this should not be permitted. It really must be an all-or-nothing agreement. A woman can't be a little bit pregnant, and a client can't be a little bit represented. If the law firm is representing the client, the firm has ultimate responsibility for the effectiveness of that representation. Not only is the client harming her own case, the reputation of the law firm is on the line. If the firm ends up looking stupid because the client was playing games, and if the firm could have avoided this by "shaking" the client out of this controlling approach, then the client's team probably is stupid.

As early as the first interview, the client must be informed of the importance of complete openness, but additionally the client must understand that nothing less is acceptable. This message in its full frontal bluntness should be presented by the lawyer dealing with the file, but it is a message that can and should be reinforced in all interviews with the client. You, as an interviewer, will probably have more client contact than the lawyer responsible for the case, and it is vital that you present a united front to the client about the type of representation your firm will be providing her.

"If the law firm is representing the client, the firm has ultimate responsibility for the effectiveness of that representation."

Lend a Helping Hand

Now here's a strange thing. Clients are more likely to contribute effectively to resolving their concerns if they like you. What's this all about? Why should liking the people you hire to resolve your legal problems matter? Strangely, it does.

You might better understand this phenomenon in this way: when you are in love, really in love, there is nothing you wouldn't do to help your chosen one. The old expression, "I would give my right arm for …" comes to mind.

Now, consider the guy who gave you the finger as he cut you off in traffic. When you see him five minutes later with his car hood up, frantically waving at you for assistance, it would take a saintly person to go to his aid.

The point? We tend to be more willing to help those people whom we like and to whom we feel close. That becomes even stronger if we perceive that our relationship is such that they will be there for us in the future.

Clients behave in a similar manner when interviewed about their legal concerns. If the client takes a liking to you, she will be attentive, interested, and cooperative. She will go out of her way to ensure that you have a clear picture of the events. She seems to care more about making your job easier. Without good rapport, your client may visibly withdraw from the interview, folding her arms and sitting back in her chair. The answers become monosyllabic and even misleading. The client can appear to adopt an attitude of "figure it out if you're so smart" or "I'm paying you to deal with this so do your job."

The stupidity of this approach is obvious. However, the client's response is an emotional one, and either the client is unaware on a conscious level of what she is doing, or unable to stop this behaviour in spite of her recognition of what is going on.

> ## "If the client takes a liking to you, she will be attentive, interested, and cooperative."

I don't mean to suggest that all clients have to like all of the people they deal with in the law firm, but it is important that, at the very least, clients do not *dislike* the people they are dealing with.

Clients need to feel comfortable in discussing the details of their legal matters; otherwise, they may withhold information. They have to have a sense that what they say matters and that you "give a damn" about them and the troubles they find themselves in. If they feel that you are receptive to them and to their perspective on the legal issues they face, clients will feel more at ease in sharing information with you.

The "strategy" of having a client feel liked and supported is not meant to be dishonest. Most people are likeable, often more likeable when they are not so stressed out by their legal woes. The particular effectiveness of this strategy is that, as you continue to work positively toward a solution to the client's legal concerns, the client becomes more likeable, they become a helpful and trusting person in your life. You reinforce them in their efforts to deal with a difficult situation, and they reinforce your sense of accomplishment at handling a difficult task well.

> ## "Working in a law office can develop your sense of self-worth, because you can be a very valuable person, making a huge contribution to 'fixing' some terrible problems, even some grave injustices."

Working in a law office can develop your sense of self-worth, because you can be a very valuable person, making a huge contribution to "fixing" some terrible problems, even some grave injustices.

Your Problem, Not Mine

When a client seeks legal advice, she is hiring the law firm based on a perception of its expertise. This is a good thing, although it brings with it a high level of responsibility. Law firms are well paid to provide excellent service and so must provide the highest level of representation to the client.

A potential pitfall here, however, is that the client may see it as the role of the law firm to "figure it all out." The client can then assume a passive role in the whole process. Somehow in this scenario, the client's legal concerns become the law firm's problems, not her own. Now, a measure of this is a good thing. The client should find a sense of relief in placing her problem in your hands and relying on your expertise. But it also can lead to the client resisting your efforts to involve her in solving the legal issues. This client may resent having to attend meetings; she may expect you to fill in gaps in the information on your own, even where the information may be at her fingertips; and she may not bother to check the information you have acquired, even when given the opportunity to review pleadings or notes from meetings.

This attitude may stem from a lack of understanding of her importance in the process or perhaps from an insecurity about her ability to assist with the legal matters. Whatever the reason, the lack of involvement by the client can be very detrimental to the potential success of her legal conflict, and it must be addressed.

From the beginning of your involvement with a client, it should be emphasized that your representation is a cooperative effort. The team tackling the client's legal matters gains its strength from how focused and smoothly it operates. Each person has a vital role in the success of the operation. The client must understand that these statements are real and not token suggestions patronizingly made to give the appearance of a client-centred approach to problem solving.

A client's true commitment to helping you help her will only come to the extent that she believes in the law firm's commitment to this approach and adopts it as her own.

Stress

The role of stress cannot be over-emphasized. It can impair the way clients function as reliable witnesses. This is a frequent phenomenon in court: a client who was clear and precise in interviews outside of court suddenly becomes a babbling fool on the stand. The responsible lawyer has to prepare a client for testimony or examinations for discovery, but as an interviewer, you should be prepared for the outbreak of incoherence to happen, even in the office.

To clients, a law office can be an intimidating place. Their initial visits are usually the first and only time they are obtaining legal advice. The mystique surrounding a law practice (and lawyers cultivate this) can be a disservice when it comes to gathering information from an overly stressed client. It may seem strange, but just being in a law office, with thoughts of the legal process sweeping over your client, can be a debilitating experience.

The stress can cause your client to blank out on dates, which causes more stress, resulting in fumbling answers, and more stress, and so on. The litigation itself may have potential outcomes that would be devastating to the client's life, and the fixation on that aspect may virtually disable the client from functioning in her normal manner. Having a client relive traumatic events can cause her to freeze or even misstate facts in surprising ways.

Naturally, one of the best ways of dealing with this situation is to make the client feel more comfortable. Creating an atmosphere of trust and acceptance is important in breaking through some of the barriers that arise in this situation. However, if you have concern for the accuracy of any information, it is your duty to check it.

> Now, you told me that you had two bottles of rye before leaving home that night.

> Did I say bottles? I meant glasses, sorry.

If a client is traumatized, it may be necessary to give her permission to emote. Simply saying to a client that she can take a few minutes to gather herself together is often enough acknowledgment of the significance of the events. It permits the client to get back on track with the interview. If it isn't sufficient time and the client needs a bit of a break, it is far better to take the break than to try to force the interview ahead with the client emotionally distracted.

> **"Whatever the reason, the lack of involvement by the client can be very detrimental to the potential success of her legal conflict, and it must be addressed."**

> **"The litigation itself may have potential outcomes that would be devastating to the client's life, and the fixation on that aspect may virtually disable the client from functioning in her normal manner."**

I heard a witness in an immigration matter who was trying to sponsor her husband to come to Canada. When asked by her counsel what her birth date was, she insisted the birth year was 1990. This would have made her 12 years old. She certainly looked to be in her early twenties, and her birth certificate showed that she was born in 1980. However, no matter how her counsel put the question to her, she kept insisting she was born in 1990. We all shrugged, and her counsel finally gave up on the effort to get her to say the right thing.

Memory problems can be an obstacle to obtaining good information from a client, even when the client has the best of intentions. It may be a momentary distraction, confusion, or simply an inability to focus at that point that fuels the memory loss. And while I always encourage a caring and empathetic approach, there is a role for a little "tough love" in an interview. You can be too lenient with a client.

Now I know you are having difficulty remembering the details, but we need to have more information to help you. I want you to go back in your mind and really work at giving me the details. I know it's hard work (or unpleasant, tiring, stressful, frustrating—pick one), but I am confident that you can help me out.

If you say, "That's OK, we can come back to that later," that suggestion can be a caring response, but it may be a little too easy. The "later" may never come, particularly if your initial interview is close to the events and therefore valuable information may be lost with a delay in the interview. For some people, memory loss is remarkably exponential over time.

Having said this, one has to be careful in breaking out the hot lights and rubber truncheons. Simply being considerate and attentive to your client's needs will go a long way in helping her relax so that she can assist you with acquiring the information your firm will need in representing her. Firmly pressing the client for more information has its place, but that technique should normally be used sparingly.

Politeness

Canadians have a reputation for being polite, but politeness has its dangers. Considerable difficulty can be created if a client, through politeness, declines to correct errors you are making in gathering information. The need to have permission to correct a mistake seems silly, but is very real for some people.

This may help explain why a client can hear you say something they know to be wrong and not correct you. Whereas, if you ask them to confirm whether you have recorded the information correctly, they will immediately show you where you went wrong.

There is a related concept that should also be kept in mind when interviewing a client, particularly for the first time. For some people, certain conversations are very difficult because of the social relationship that exists. For example, a man may have difficulty discussing certain things with a young woman, particularly if the topic may make him seem less "manly." Likewise, a woman may not want to discuss intimate matters with a man she barely knows. A young person may not feel comfortable with an adult but be able to discuss matters freely with his peers. Age, sex, religion—there are many barriers to open communication. You can allow these obstacles to thwart your interview, or you can work to overcome them.

You must find ways to deal with a client's "interview resistance." A rare instance of terminating an interview because a client is uncomfortable with an interviewer is not a serious problem. However, if it happens frequently, the law firm will have to consider having someone handle the interviewing who can deal with the clients more effectively.

Developing rapport with the client, using empathic interventions in the interview, confirming the importance of having all the correct information, and simply being a good listener will all help in this task. And you can use the force of your magnetic personality to persuade clients to confide in you.

On the other hand, ignoring the obstacle will not work. If there is a problem that interferes with your communication with the client, put it on the table and deal with it!

> *I notice that you are somewhat nervous about discussing this topic. We do need to have a clear picture of what happened. Is there something I can do to help you talk about this?*
>
> No … it's just that … well, it's difficult to talk about with a … girl.
>
> *Well, it's nice to know someone still thinks of me as a girl, but you should know that I have been dealing with matters like this for a lot of years and I think I can safely say that nothing you will tell me will be upsetting or embarrassing to me. Why don't you just close your eyes and imagine you are talking to a 280-pound truck driver.*

A little humour will usually help, but you must make a concerted effort to help the client through this block. You may be dealing with a client over a number of years, and you can't go running for help every time something uncomfortable crops up.

What's That Got To Do with Anything?

Many clients will screen out information, not because they are worried about how it will look for them, but simply because they don't think it is important. The importance might be obvious to a person with legal training, but not to the client. When the importance becomes obvious, the lawyer might ask the client, "Why didn't you tell me that before?" The typical answer to that question is, "You never asked." This scenario will often present itself when dealing with the controlling client, but is not limited to that personality type.

Lawyers conducting interviews will often strive to limit the amount of talk from the client. This stems from a fear of the babbling brook that can't be stopped and the common experience that lawyers have that there simply isn't enough time to do everything. It may also point to an arrogance that says, "I know what is important so I'll ask the right questions and you limit your answers to those brilliant and insightful questions."

The combined effect of the client limiting herself by screening out information that she deems irrelevant and the interviewer limiting the client by narrowly programming the question–answer process is almost certainly guaranteed to lose valuable information.

To overcome these obstacles, it is important, particularly in the early stages of fact gathering, to invite the client to provide as much information as possible. The

> **"Many clients will screen out information, not because they are worried about how it will look for them, but simply because they don't think it is important."**

client should be encouraged to tell you everything about the incident(s), without worrying about screening out information. You can assure her that you will be capable of determining what is important from the body of information she provides.

Generally speaking, clients can be trusted to make intelligent decisions about what is relevant to their legal concerns.

In some instances you can appeal to your client's better instincts: she might be more inclined to provide full particulars if she understands the importance of the information that you are requesting. If she realizes the benefits of having good information (and the problems created by poor information), she may see the advantage to herself and work harder at her job of assisting with information gathering.

Occasionally, you will need information from an interviewee to help someone else out—for example, if you are interviewing a witness who saw an accident where your client was injured as a result of another person's negligence. The appeal to a witness's civic spirit is not entirely lost, even in today's cynical world. These approaches are probably more useful and necessary in your role as a paralegal than as a lawyer.

Personality

> **"The client should be encouraged to tell you everything about the incident(s), without worrying about screening out information."**

All other factors aside, there could be just that "something" indefinable between you and your client that just doesn't click. It may sound easier said than done, but you have to rise above those feelings. People under stress often do not exhibit their best side. You must draw upon the calm, caring part of yourself and not react to those traits or actions in this person that seem to bait you. If you don't have a calm caring part in you, then borrow it for the length of the interview. You are a professional and, like a doctor who doesn't get to choose whom she treats, you must work with everyone the firm represents.

If you can't bring yourself to conduct interviews in an open and sensitive way, then that is an issue between you and the law firm. You are, quite frankly, less valuable as an employee if you are not able to provide excellent service to all the firm's clients.

There may be aspects of your personality that could cause unwanted reactions from some clients. You may strike the client as too abrupt, impatient, distant, hostile—any number of less-than-flattering characterizations. While learning to be a good interviewer, part of the necessary introspection that you must do is to understand how you appear to others. This is particularly important when it comes to persons that you meet professionally, clients most of all.

You can pursue your understanding in this area through practice and feedback, open discussions with lawyers or other personnel who observe you doing interviewing from time to time, and even from conversations with clients. Having a frank discussion with the client as to how she felt about the interview can, in fact, help to overcome any negative reactions she may have had during the interview process. It can also open up lines of communication, helping you to work more effectively with the client.

Part of your job is to keep options open with clients. Developing solutions is up to the lawyer to work on with the client. Your contribution to this process is to accumulate information that will fuel the advice leading to those solutions, to ensure that the client is comfortable with your involvement in the process, and to encourage the client to keep an open mind about strategies and expected outcomes.

Appendix B lists various obstacles to client communication, possible explanations for them, and some suggested tactics to overcome them. Appendix C lists the main types of avoidance responses people employ with some suggestions as to why clients use them, and a few tactics that interviewers can use to deal with them.

To end on a positive note: I am sure you will be able to overcome the petty annoyances that will surface as you learn to be a legal interviewer. You are clearly an intelligent and adaptable person or you would not be where you are now.

"You are a professional and, like a doctor who doesn't get to choose whom she treats, you must work with everyone the firm

CHAPTER QUESTIONS

1. Outline four factors that can impair a client's ability to talk openly about her legal issues.

2. What two elements of initial client contact are important for you, the interviewer, to do well?

3. Why is it important to deal with the emotional aspects of a client's concerns?

CHAPTER EXERCISE

In your interactions with people over the next week, both at work and in your non-work life, observe how both of you are interacting. Consider the motivation behind each person's approach to his or her behaviour and talk. Consider the effectiveness or ineffectiveness of each person's approach.

CHAPTER 2

Interview Preparation

In Brief

This chapter discusses interview preparation and the importance of developing rapport with the client from the earliest stages.

> An interview is two or more persons talking—with the object of exchanging information.

An interview can be an informal chat with a friend. On a professional basis, interviews are conducted by doctors, lawyers, bankers, dentists, and plumbers. It could be for a job or with someone who is helping you put together a resume.

Interviews take various shapes and forms, differing in their formality, seriousness, equality of participation, structure, and length. A police interrogation, for example, is an interview, but the suspect may feel he has little choice about participating. Here, there is an enormous power imbalance, and he may be inclined—particularly if he has had legal advice—to "clam up." At the other end of the scale, two people meeting for the first time through a matchmaking service will be motivated to create a favourable impression; both are interested in giving and getting information; both are on a relatively equal footing. Interestingly, the outcome in each of these examples can be equally important in the lives of the participants.

One note of caution: if you are meeting with someone to explore a romantic relationship and you are asked to sit in a hard chair, under an intense light, while answering questions put to you in an angry or hostile manner, you might want to get your fee back from the matchmaking service.

Interviews are usually an exchange between two people, one of whom has a formal, information-gathering task. There are group interviews, but they are usually little more than a sequence of one-on-one interviews, often with the interviewers taking responsibility for a specific area, with pre-screened questions. The value here is that, for the period of time, while one interviewer is asking questions, the others can step back from the process and concentrate on the interviewee, his body language, the nuances of his "performance." Job applicants are sometimes subject to the process of a group interview. It can be an intimidating experience.

An interview can have a variety of objectives, and each type demands or presupposes certain methods. Figure 2.1 outlines the basic types, with examples and methods for each.

In the context of a legal interview, a second person often attends with a client. This may be a parent (when a child is being interviewed), a spouse, or an interested relative or friend. This variation will be discussed later, under the heading of conflicts, but you should make certain that, if you proceed with an interview with a third party present, you have determined that your client has freely chosen to be accompanied and that issues of compromised confidentiality have been explored.

Since most interviews usually comprise two people, it is necessary to look at the interaction between the two, as well as how each individual functions. If you have ever tried to communicate with a person who is giving you the "silent treatment," you understand that both people need to be involved in the process for any meaningful communication to happen.

In considering the range of interview styles, it may be helpful to look at interviews on a continuum from least formal to most formal, as outlined in figure 2.2.

Interviewing a client in a law office is moderately formal. It should not induce the dread that some people feel about visits to their dentist; however, clients tend to be nervous when dealing with lawyers—legal concerns are costly in terms of time, money, and emotions. Information fuels legal representation, and poor information directly translates into poor results. So how do you ensure that the information you are obtaining is the "good stuff"? By applying the techniques outlined in this book, you should be able, consistently, to obtain high-quality information from your interviews.

FEATURES OF A GOOD INTERVIEW

1. *Preparation*: Know where you are going. A clearly defined objective and a plan for how to reach it will go a long way to ensuring a successful interview.

2. *Client rapport*: A client who is comfortable with the process, trusts your competence, and feels that you will deal sensitively with their legal matters will be very helpful to you in accumulating the information you require.

3. *Style of questioning*: The right approach to questioning the client will facilitate his opening up to you and encourage a team-work approach to resolving his legal concerns.

4. *Thoroughness*: By fully exploring the legal issues, your firm will be on solid ground in representing the client. Surprises will be rare, and lost time from pursuing "red herrings" will be minimized.

Figure 2.1   Interview Objectives

Objective	Examples	Methods
Gathering information	survey, aspects of legal interviewing	various types of questions, written surveys, or questionnaires
Dispensing information/ advocating	press release, advertising pitch, tribunal representation	verbal, written, various media
Resolving problems/ therapeutic	counsellor, medical exam, aspects of legal interviewing	open-ended questioning, values clarification, advice
Assessment/appraisal	job evaluation, property appraisal, oral exam	gathering information from various sources, directive or challenging questions
Stress appraisal	physical evaluation, practical exam, Outward Bound	creation of a challenge or obstacle for the subject to overcome, and observe how the person reacts to the challenge

Figure 2.2   Interview Styles

	Informal	Moderately formal	Formal
Characteristics	• intimate and unstructured • equal stature of participants • free-flowing topics • loose time constraints • flexible process • no set purpose	• relatively structured • some hierarchy • set area of discussion • time limited • clearly defined process • objective understood by participants	• highly structured • great disparity in power • agenda predetermined by more powerful party • time frame controlled by one party • rigid process • objective controlled by more powerful party and may be hidden from weaker party
Examples	• chat with a neighbour • bump into a friend at the mall • pillow talk	• job interview • legal interview • doctor's examination • telephone survey • debate	• press conference • police interrogation • religious revival • tax audit

PRE-INTERVIEW PREPARATION

Preparation is key to a good interview. Unlike many interviews (such as those conducted by a doctor, clergy member, or therapist), you usually know the general area of law the client is seeking help with. You know if they are coming to see you about a motor vehicle accident, the purchase of a house, or the preparation of a will. This is a great advantage, but it carries some dangers. Some lawyers immediately begin firing questions at the client to maximize their efficiency, to get the heart of the issue in the shortest possible time. Given that lawyers quickly develop an expertise in a particular area of law, it is not surprising that they feel like they know the right questions to ask, what needs to be done on any particular file.

"Information fuels legal representation."

One study of doctors interviewing patients determined that the average time a doctor listened to his patient before beginning to dispense advice was something like 31 seconds. While most lawyers would not be giving advice in that time frame, they would usually be firing very specific questions by then. There is more about questioning techniques in chapter 6, but the importance of letting a client tell his story—in an uninterrupted manner—can't be emphasized too much.

What kind of preparation is required for an interview? To some extent, it depends upon the type of interview, but generally you should know the legal issues and be aware of the next logical steps for the client to take. Here are some things to think about as you are preparing for the upcoming interview.

"An organized structure superimposed over the interview not only ensures that the necessary information is obtained from the client, but can also be very impressive to the client when he sees the thought that has gone into the process."

1. Know what you are trying to achieve.

2. Prepare a plan or agenda.

3. Let the client in on the plan.

4. Map with the client where you are as you proceed through the agenda. Mapping is a good metaphor since you may need to detour along the way—flexibility is one key to a good interview.

Mr. Jones, we have about 40 minutes today to do this interview. What I would like to do is have you describe how the investment in Drywell Oil came about. I will have some specific questions for you, once you have outlined the events that bring you here today, and you will have an opportunity to add any comments or ask questions before we conclude.

After the interview, we will both have some tasks to complete. I will write up a memo for the lawyer, and you will receive a copy to review to ensure that my summary is accurate.

Any questions at this point? … No? … Then please tell me what you remember, and please be as thorough as possible. In a legal action, details, even small ones, can be important.

Planning ahead does not mean that the interview should be pre-scripted. You need to listen to what the client has come to say. Planning merely implies that you should have a good sense of what information will likely be required in order to proceed to the next stages in representing the client. At all times, flexibility in accommodating a client's circumstance is essential. During the interview, you need to remain open to unusual or unexpected situations. You will miss important details if you approach the interview with blinders on, failing to see an important issue hovering in your peripheral vision.

Your law firm will often have checklists or questionnaires available that can form a basis for the interview. It is usually preferable to interview the client and complete the checklist yourself. Resist the urge to let clients fill it out on their own, while you just give it the once-over. Clients seldom appreciate the nuances and significance of what may appear to be minor points. You, however, must be aware of the purpose and significance of each question, whether it is on a form or something that arises during an interview. And running through the list of questions mechanically is not much better than leaving the client to answer the questions on his own. It can also alienate your client.

One thing that is often overlooked in interviews is the concept of mitigation—that is, anyone who has suffered an injury is obliged to take reasonable steps to limit the extent of the damages arising from the injury. For example, if you are injured, you must seek the appropriate medical help and follow the advice of your medical practitioner. If you are wrongfully terminated from your job, you must seek other employment, thus reducing your wage-loss claim. To the extent that you do not try to mitigate your damages, a court may well reduce your award. So, what implications does this have for your client's interview? Knowing that your client is required to mitigate, as an interviewer you would ask questions designed to explore the efforts made by the client to lessen his damages. It may be, for example, that the client has been told by his doctor to exercise regularly, but he has not been able to because he slipped and re-injured himself. If the doctor is unaware of this re-injury, she may think that your client has not taken reasonable steps to remedy his medical problems and this impression may reflect badly on your client. By documenting this information and perhaps bringing it to the lawyer's attention, you will be providing an important service to the client.

Sort the information into logical headings, and discuss each heading in a conversational manner, eliciting the detail that you require. For example, in dealing with a motor vehicle accident, you would have headings such as: *description of accident, extent of injuries, treatment received, financial repercussions,* etc. It is important to consider these categories ahead of time and to prepare questions to ask under each heading. Using a flexible approach, however, you, the interviewer, would discuss each area and probe for the sort of detail you require in a manner where the interview flows logically.

As a starter, you may find it helpful to look at appendix D for a general checklist for interviews.

An organized structure not only ensures that the necessary information is obtained from the client, but can also be very impressive to the client when he sees the thought that has gone into the process. You can accomplish this by outlining, to the client, how the interview will be conducted.

First, I will ask you to describe for me how the motor vehicle accident happened, then we will discuss the injuries you sustained. Later, we will discuss your treatment and the financial consequences of the accident. Finally, I will want to listen to any concerns you have that should be brought to the lawyer's attention.

What is even more impressive is when you actually follow this outline, letting the client know where you are on the road map as you go.

Do you have any further information to add regarding how the accident happened?

No, that about covers it.

Any questions at this stage?

No, thank you.

All right, let's now move on to discuss the injuries you sustained.

With this approach, the client feels that you really know what you are doing and where you are going—like you have done this "stuff" before. To the greatest extent possible, your client should feel like the advertisement says, "You're in good hands with … ."

In addition to checklists, when you are new to an area of law, you can gain valuable information from looking at the pleadings in a related file. A statement of claim in a wrongful dismissal action will have content that is particular to the client's claim—and also more general aspects that are necessary for any wrongful dismissal action to succeed. The same is true in a divorce matter: the proper names of the parties; names and birthdates of the children; when and where the marriage took place; and when, where, and how it broke down are all matters that will have to be dealt with in any action. This can form the basis of a self-generated checklist.

Of course, most checklists won't contain a question about whether the client's spouse was recently charged with selling child pornography on the Web, or if the client's spouse receives correspondence from some bank in the Bahamas. This is why it is important to ask some broad general questions that will coax the client to think of any helpful information that is not covered by the narrow checklist.

In other words, know what you are looking for, but don't become so wedded to the expected answers that you miss unusual content.

CLIENT RAPPORT

The concept of client rapport should not be confused with liking your client. If law firms only represented likeable people, many people would be without legal representation. At the same time, a client must not have a sense that you or the lawyer dislikes him. That is too much to swallow when he is paying a high hourly rate for the service provided. Rapport is also not the same as empathy, which we discuss elsewhere. Rapport just implies that the client feels comfortable communicating and doesn't have to struggle getting his meaning across.

One of the most effective ways to establish rapport with a client is to listen. And to be sure that your client knows you are listening, you need to use verbal and non-verbal cues. In client-centred legal interviewing, remember that the client is the boss. He pays the bills and instructs the lawyer; the lawyer simply advises. Your client needs to understand this relationship; otherwise, he may take the approach of withdrawing his input and letting the experts do it. This *sit back and see what transpires* approach eliminates half of the dynamic duo—the client and the lawyer working together.

Sometimes when clients come to seek legal assistance, they have been used and abused terribly. They may have a low self-concept as a result of victimization or they may feel, in spite of seeking legal help, that it is pointless to oppose the forces aligned against them. To help change this kind of perspective, it is helpful to involve the client in the process of legal representation. Clients need to have a feeling of personal empowerment, and this can be achieved, partly by the lawyer informing them of their legal rights, but mostly by the way they are treated by the law firm's staff. Conveying the message that your client is a crucial member of the team will help to bring him on board and strengthen the legal representation that he receives.

Many law firms are intimidating in their physical layout and hierarchical structure. The lawyer's office is designed to impress; just as court rooms emphasize the importance of the commanding figure at the top, law offices are often set up so that the client must run a gauntlet of "lesser" persons before reaching the lawyer's inner sanctum. She is often seated behind a huge oak desk, occupying a dark leather chair, the biggest and most comfortable one in the office. While you won't have quite the same opulence, the aura of superiority can rub off on you. Rather than basking in this, you need to break down this barrier to client participation, to humanize the law firm for your client.

The language you use can either reinforce the "we're the experts, sit back and watch us do our stuff" approach or invite the client to be part of the team working on his behalf. The team analogy is helpful, and it doesn't hurt to use it with the client. Figure 2.3 presents a contrast between non-empowering and empowering language.

> *We'd like to approach resolving your legal concerns as a team, and you are an important part of that team.*

"It is far more important that the client's anxiety be dealt with right off, rather than for it to worry its way into his relationship with your firm."

This statement can just be lip service, if the working relationship with the client does not reflect the philosophy expressed. Telling the client "just sign these medical releases where indicated" places the client on the receiving end of commands. Compare that tactic with explaining the form and asking him if he is comfortable signing it. It is the client who must be satisfied and comfortable with the process. Some anxiety may accompany this process: your client may say he is not comfortable signing the medical release. What do you do then? Well, you deal with the discomfort. Perhaps he is concerned that sensitive medical information that has nothing to do with the litigation will be released to the other side. There is a mechanism for dealing with this, and it is far more important that the client's anxiety be dealt with right off, rather than for it to worry its way into his relationship with your firm.

Some less experienced interviewers feel the need to impress the client with the depth of their knowledge. Normally, this is just tiresome, but in some instances it can actually damage your relations with your client. If a client asks you a question that you do not know the answer to, don't fake it. Your chances of getting caught are high, and if your client suspects BS, you risk everything. Acknowledge that you do not know the answer, and tell him that you will find it out or have his lawyer address the issue. This can be done with strength and confidence, and it will actually reinforce the client's perception of you as a capable person.

Remember that while you are evaluating the client, he is also evaluating you. We all know people who have a great need to impress, and these people are universally unimpressive. The more a person tries to con us with their importance, the less esteem he acquires. Be real. Be honest with clients. You really do have a lot to offer them, and you should be confident in that knowledge.

How you approach a client when conducting interviews will have an enormous impact on your relationship with him over the months and even years that your firm may represent him. Always keep in mind that you can have a powerful influence over the client, an impact which either makes him feel positive about the representation he receives or uneasy and unhappy with it.

"Today you are going to give me information about your workers' compensation claim." Saying that can make the client feel exactly like he felt when dealing with the bureaucrat who caused the problem. Rather, you could say:

Figure 2.3   Language of Empowerment

Non-empowering	Empowering
What we will do today …	The way I would like to approach our meeting … Would it be all right with you if we …
I need information on …	It would help if you can assist me with … I would like to get information on …
Tell me about the attack.	I know this is painful to remember, but are you comfortable with discussing the attack? Are you able to talk about the attack at this point?
Next we will deal with …	Are you ready to move on to … Is it all right with you if we discuss …
That's all I need for today.	Is there anything further that you wish to discuss?
Give me more detail on that point.	Can you help me understand that a bit better?
Your answer isn't very clear.	I haven't quite got what you mean by that. I'm sorry, somehow your meaning has escaped me.
We only have time to deal with …	Can you help me prioritize …

It would be helpful for us today to discuss your WCB claim and your concerns about it. Is that all right with you?

Of course your client is not likely to say, "No, I don't want to talk about what brought me to your firm in the first place," but the language you use in introducing this topic conveys a message: *your permission is needed and your help is valued.*

By approaching matters this way, and if you do have to touch on a sensitive topic, *how this accident has affected your sex life*, your client will be more comfortable telling you that he is not ready to discuss this right now. As important, he will likely feel more comfortable talking about it simply because you have given him permission not to.

To establish a good rapport, you should be sensitive to a client's use of language and level of comfort in dealing with both written and oral communications. Communication is about language, whether spoken or unspoken. Working in a law office can—and probably will—make you very comfortable with uncommon vocabulary. Amongst the other legal workers, the language we use can incorporate legalese, if that helps to communicate a specific message. This same language may not work with clients. Clients need to understand what we tell them and respond appropriately to questions we ask, so they need to understand us. It is of no value to impress a client with a 50-dollar word if, in the end, the client misconstrues our meaning. Often, clients will not stop us to inquire about a term we use; they are shy to do so, not wanting us to think they are stupid.

> *I am glad you came to us, Mr. Jones. This issue requires the utmost dispatch. I preface my assurances with a few caveats but I believe that with a modicum of fortuitousness we will be successful in securing your chattels. We will need to draft a statement of claim, file liens, execute some other documents and attend to service expeditiously, but in my humble opinion an action in replevin is the way to go. Any questions?*

What the lawyer has said, of course, is that if we act quickly and file the right documents, with a bit of luck we can get your stuff back. Of course the client is unlikely to understand this and is almost as unlikely to ask for clarification. The process, like the Catholic church before Luther, will be shrouded in mystery, unwelcoming to the common person.

Monitor your language. Check with the client to ensure that he understands what you have said; in some instances, you can ask him to summarize his understanding of what you have said. You may be surprised by what he says.

If there is a simple way to say it, use those words; if not, provide a translation as you go. "The document refers to an action in replevin, that is an application to the court to recover goods taken from you." And you should not make the client ask for explanations, even sophisticated clients can miss the meaning in obscure language and never stop you to ask for clarification.

The law should be accessible to all people, so anything worth saying is worth saying simply.

"The law should be accessible to all people, so anything worth saying is worth saying simply."

Think about rapport. Make a conscious attempt to put your client at ease with your greeting, the atmosphere you create, and your attentiveness to him. Many of the things you do, like offering coffee or juice, giving a warm greeting and hand-shake, or assisting a client with his chair, are not strictly necessary. The client is often aware that this is all part of a conscious gesture of openness. Even so, he will generally like the gesture precisely because it shows that you are attending to his needs, that you care about his comfort, and that you want him to feel positive about his encounter with your law office. In many instances the fact that you thought to make the gesture outweighs the physical effect of the gesture. It's the thought that counts.

There used to be a program on television called *The Commish*. The rather bizarre premise of this program was that the lead character, who was the commissioner of police, would become involved in police investigations. In one episode, he was at the home of a woman who had been sexually assaulted. The police were on the scene investigating and, as you might imagine, there were a huge number of officers wandering about the house—big men in blue, with all their gear and imposing presence, going about their job of collecting evidence. As the Commish arrives, the victim is sitting in her living room, surrounded by investigators, with this chaos swirling about her. She looks withdrawn, abused, a cowering animal. The Commish takes a trainee officer in tow and says, "Watch how this situation should be dealt with." He then proceeds to interview the victim.

Standing in front of her, he starts to ask his first question and then interrupts himself saying something like, "I'm sorry, it's been a long day. Would you mind if I sat down to talk with you?" Naturally, she gives permission. The other officers have been sitting, standing, moving about as they please. The request surprises her. He again starts to ask a question, but once more pauses. He looks down at the candy dish on the coffee table and says, "I'm

afraid I haven't had a chance to eat dinner. Would you mind if I had a candy?" The victim obliges and on it goes. The point here is that the Commish is demonstrating a simple and some-what subtle mechanism to empower the victim. She has been assaulted in her own home, her former place of power, where she thought she had control over her life.

When the police come, typically they further reduce her power by clomping around her house, looking through her personal effects, poking and prodding her with intrusive questions. The process, intended to help the victim, results in her further victimization. When the victim is given back a measure of control over her living space ("May I sit down?") and her possessions ("May I have a candy?"), the long and pain-filled process of rebuilding her person begins. From the point of view of the inter-viewer, the victim starts to be empow-ered to help herself, the first stage of which is to provide information to the police that will aid them in finding her attacker. The stronger she is, the more help she will be to the police in doing their job. This is teamwork, not unlike what takes place in legal interviewing, where the client is often feeling abused and victimized.

CHAPTER QUESTIONS

1. How would you define interviewing?

2. Give an example of a formal interview and an example of an informal one.

3. What is "mapping" in the context of interviewing?

4. How can you effectively develop rapport with a client?

CHAPTER EXERCISES

1. Look again at figure 2.3, which deals with the language of empowerment. Create five more examples of non-empowering statements, then indicate how they could be changed into empowering statements.

2. Think about the last three interviews you have had—with a doctor, accountant, parent, academic counsellor, etc. Do you recall any moments when you were uncertain about what was happening? Did you feel free to question the interviewer? Is there any way the interviewer could have made you more comfortable? Could she have made the process more open to you?

CHAPTER 3

Structure of the Interview

In Brief

This chapter explores the structure of the interview. Not surprisingly, it consists of a beginning, middle, and end. The discussion includes some approaches to take at the various stages, with emphasis on the importance of a personalized style of interviewing.

To be the best you can be at the task of legal interviewing, you need, eventually, to develop a style of your own, one that is consistent with your own comfort level and strengths. Not all interviewers will be equally good at dealing with all aspects or stages of an interview. However, it is possible to create an approach that best suits your own skill level and maximizes the useful information you obtain from your client. Not every approach or style is equally valid and useful, but you should look at the suggestions made in this book as guidelines. You can vary the approaches outlined, but you should do so for a good reason. You need to feel comfortable that the results produce positive gains in the quality and amount of information that you obtain and the satisfaction your client has with her involvement with your firm.

The interview process has logical steps in its natural life. By pointing out the obvious, I hope that you will consider these steps and develop each stage in a manner you can be comfortable with and that nets effective results in the client interview. The stages of an interview can be broken down as follows:

1. Pre-interview preparation

2. Commencement of the interview—client orientation

3. Body of the interview/fact gathering

4. Winding down the interview

5. Follow-up

PRE-INTERVIEW PREPARATION

The pre-interview preparation ensures that you are ready to deal with the client, to maximize the quality and quantity of information obtained in the interview, as well as being sure that the client leaves the interview feeling satisfied that the law firm has the situation well in hand. The pre-interview process was outlined in chapter 2 and is discussed in detail in chapter 4.

COMMENCEMENT

The secretary tells you that the client has now arrived and is in the waiting area. At this point, a series of choices begins. These choices can be conscious or subliminal, but they are very real and affect your interview in a very real manner.

Do You Ask the Secretary To Send the Client in or Do You Go and Fetch the Client?

This will depend on a number of factors. Is it the client's first visit? If so, will she be able to find your office?—you may *need* to go to the waiting room to greet the client. Depending on the layout of the office, you may *wish* to do so at any rate.

I once went for a meeting with a lawyer, and when I got off the elevator I went to a reception area. The lawyer came to get me, and I followed him along seemingly endless, winding corridors to a small boardroom. I likely could never have followed directions and gotten to the right room. Interestingly, after the meeting, we left the boardroom, and the lawyer took two steps and opened a door leading to the elevators. For security reasons the law firm didn't want clients and others wandering around the office, but instead funnelled everyone past reception. That the lawyer came to greet me, in this instance, was more a function of logistics and security than courtesy, but it served both purposes well. He and I exchanged small talk while wending a path through a busy legal jungle, and I felt personally attended to. Even when you are dealing with an old and trusted client, usually the best thing is to go and collect her.

The added attention and consideration shown to your client will give her a sense of how important she is to your firm as well as your desire to foster the relationship. Thus, greeting the client in the reception area is as appropriate whether it is a first visit or a twentieth.

Other factors argue in favour of fetching the client from reception. If the client is brought to your office, she may arrive when you are in the middle of something else. Another client's file open on your desk can be awkward, and it may result in confidentiality breaches. If you are in the middle of a telephone conversation, you may then have two clients with legitimate concerns about confidentiality. It is best to clear the track so you can devote your entire attention to the client and ensure that you will not be interrupted in your meeting. A separate space or room for the meeting can be an excellent idea, since it can ensure privacy, lack of interruption, and avoid any inadvertent lapses in confidentiality.

brought her to your office. Then there is the questioning and clarification phase. Then you provide an opportunity for the client to supplement what she has told you. Finally, in closing, you present a plan for what steps will be taken next.

In orienting the client, then, it makes sense to tell the client, at the beginning, the approach you will be taking. The client will then know it is her task to tell you everything that she thinks is important, that you will question her in detail, and that she will have an opportunity to ask questions or supplement the information, before the two of you agree on what the next steps will be. This is of great assistance to your client: she can organize her thoughts to assist the lawyer, who can then provide a clear and concise outline of the legal issue.

BODY OF THE INTERVIEW

Let the client talk! Most interviewing experts suggest this. However, many lawyers begin their interviews in precisely the opposite way. This is discussed further in chapter 6.

Firing a series of narrow and pointed questions at the client may impress her about how much you know about the law; however, it often leads to incorrect data, and important information goes missing. This can result in the law firm pursuing a strategy based on mistaken assumptions, which will lead to costly misadventures. Sometimes the missteps are irrevocably disastrous.

> "The interviewer is facilitating the telling of a story to try to ensure completeness and accuracy, not directing a play."

During this stage, the interviewer should remember he is getting information, not giving it. In whatever manner feels most appropriate and comfortable, invite your clients to tell you why they are seeking legal advice. They know why they have come to a law firm, and, given a chance, they will tell you.

Talk-show host Vicki Gabereau reports that her father always told her she had two ears and one mouth—the proportion of time she should be listening to the time she should be talking.

The interviewer is facilitating the telling of a story to try to ensure completeness and accuracy, not directing a play. The content must come from the client. Resist the temptation to fill in blanks when a client pauses, to make assumptions about what the client means, to "help" the client out by proposing statements to which they only have to agree. Clients have been living with their legal concerns, often for years—they have mentally run through the scenarios a multitude of times, and they have usually distilled the important facts so that they can summarize the issue in a few minutes. The greatest temptation at this stage is to interrupt the client, perhaps to assure her that you know a lot about the area of law concerned. Don't.

At this stage, you need to remain relatively neutral and non-judgmental. Just listen to the client's information. I say relatively neutral, because you also want to reassure the client that you are acting for her, that you are on her side. Your client must know that the law firm appreciates her position and will do whatever it can to achieve the best results. Being non-judgmental gives your client the trust that she can say whatever she needs to and not have to deal with emotional or legal fallout from someone who may morally disagree with her position. The legal issues alone may impact on how she lives the rest of her life; she has to know that you are not there to judge her. Some expressions that sound supportive but are quite neutral include, "Good, tell me more," or "That's helpful information"—where it is the *giving* of information that is being positively commented on, not really the *content* of the client's information. Nevertheless, the client feels that she is being supported and is in attentive hands.

As the interview progresses, you may find it necessary to focus or refocus the interview. As the interviewer, you know what kind of information is needed. You can—or may have to—ask your client to clarify or expand on particular answers. And you need to remember not to be so focused on one issue that you ignore or forget other, more important questions. The expression "He can't see the forest for the trees" comes to mind.

FACT GATHERING

Legal actions run on detail. For the most part, the nature of a lawyer's job dictates the extensive detail he needs to know. As a legal professional, you must have a voracious appetite for detail.

For the client, important aspects have (often, long ago) been identified, considered and reconsidered, and analyzed from almost every conceivable perspective. Using a client-centred approach, you have invited the client to tell her story. Usually, the key elements have been succinctly identified by the client within about five minutes. Don't stop there. The tendency, almost compulsion by lawyers and their staff, is to then begin the series of narrow, directive questions. *Resist, resist, resist.*

This is the most dangerous path the interviewer can take. It has enormous potential to overlook and mislead. This route is controlled by the interviewer's assumptions and biases. The process of drawing out information from the client becomes subtly corrupted by what the interviewer wants to hear, thinks she will hear, or what the client thinks the interviewer wants to hear.

This initial part of the process is often referred to as "preliminary problem identification," and it is vital that the law firm have a complete understanding of the client's legal concerns before carrying on. Yes, the interviewer must dig for detail, but don't launch into narrow questions quite yet. This will initially feel like having one hand tied behind your back. Don't worry, the feeling will pass, and as an interviewer you will be stronger for it.

Interviews are sometimes categorized as either directive or non-directive, terms perhaps more suited to social or therapeutic interviews. In directive interviews, the interviewer sets the topic, pace, location, and any other significant aspects of the interview and the interviewee is limited to being responsive or reactive. In a non-directive interview, the interviewer, to a great extent, leaves it to the client to determine the content, to set the pace, possibly even determine the location of the interview. The idea behind this approach is that it invites the client to select what is important and provide information that she is comfortable sharing. For example, an interview conducted at the client's home will have a very different feel from one conducted at a law office.

In the context of a legal interview, neither a strictly directive or non-directive approach works well. However, by combining these approaches, you can achieve an appropriate level of client comfort and obtain the necessary information. The interviewer can choose legally relevant issues but ask open-ended questions, and the client can tell what she feels is important. Drawing a client out about her legal issues is an art and skill well worth developing.

Tell me how the argument started.

Ultimately, you will be responsible for obtaining the necessary information from the client. However, the interviewer must give the client the opportunity to define what is important. The interviewer on her own would often overlook aspects that are not just emotionally important to clients but that have great legal significance to resolving their concerns.

You should follow up your initial open question by encouraging the client to tell you more. Seldom will the client give you enough information on the first pass to allow you to plot out a viable legal strategy. Having invited the client to tell you about her concerns, encourage her to elaborate on what she has told you. As with most things, the direct approach is often the best.

Can you tell me more about that?

Could you give me some more detail about what happened?

I once represented a client on a personal injury case. In an examination for discovery, the opposing lawyer, acting for the insurer, questioned the client about her injuries. He did a typical thing of starting from the toes and working up the body, asking whether there were any injuries in each region. What he did do with such thoroughness, unlike anything I'd witnessed, was to repeatedly ask whether there was anything else that the client had suffered from. So, he would ask the client to tell him about the extent of the injury to her hip. She would comment on that until she didn't appear to have anything more to say. He would then ask, is there anything else in relation to your hip? The client most often said no, but occasionally added a comment. He would then say, are you sure? and the client would emphatically say, "Yes, I am sure." What this lawyer accomplished was to give himself the assurance that the injured person could not come back, later, with another complaint that had not been listed, without seriously tarnishing her credibility. This was a very good service to his client, the insurer.

Having told her story, your client often will then mentally review it, remembering details that were left out in the first go round. She will likely welcome the opportunity to fill in the gaps with these points—points that often are key to proper legal representation. As an interviewer, you can't possibly read the client's mind, so by immediately pursuing details about the initial revelations, you will almost certainly miss out on important facts. After the initial interview, these important facts can become buried in the hustle and bustle of litigation, in response to demands from the other side, and in other changing circumstances, only to rear their ugly heads at the worst possible moment.

There will be time enough for narrow or closed questioning; the initial stages are for identifying the range and nuances of a client's concerns. Legal representation has frequently been treated much like ordering from a menu in a diner. *I'll have the number 11.* If the diner is busy and noisy, the customer may get a number 7 instead—not a very satisfying experience. Too often, lawyers and their assistants make assumptions about what the client's issues are, without enough background information to appreciate this particular client's specific concerns. The client who requires a number 11—and is served a number 7 by the law firm—will not be satisfied and may well not return for a second serving.

Once you have a *full* appreciation for the client's situation, then intelligent, direct questioning can provide the minute detail required to follow up in the interests of the client. When you know enough about the relevant area of law, you can obtain the dates, places, times, etc., so that the paperwork can be properly completed. That is the time and the place for checklists. By focusing on this detail too early, you run the enormous risk of losing the big picture. As they say, the devil is in the details.

STYLE OF QUESTIONING

In chapter 6, "Questioning Techniques," the issue of approaches to questioning will be thoroughly examined; however, keep in mind now that there is a strategy to questioning. The interviewer does not simply pop out the next thought or question that enters his head. In addition, be mindful that a particular questioning approach that is appropriate with one client may be quite unproductive with another.

Different questioning styles are called for at different stages in the interview. You may question a client differently, depending on how well you know her and

Some years ago, a client hired me to assist with her Dalkon Shield claim. As you may recall, the Dalkon Shield birth-control device caused considerable complications for women using it. Some of the women required painful medical interventions, and many women became sterile from the side-effects of its use.

About 20 years had passed since my client's intrauterine device (IUD) had been removed in an emergency operation. The hospital had destroyed most of their records of the operation; the remaining files gave no indication of which IUD had been removed from the patient. The doctor who performed the operation had been retired for about four years. Getting beyond the first stage in the process, establishing that it was a Dalkon Shield that caused her problems, did not look promising. I contacted the doctor and asked him if he could remember which IUD had been used by my client. He politely informed me that, having performed thousands of minor operations, he couldn't possibly remember 20-year-old details. I was persistent and asked the doctor to allow me to show him the limited records that I had obtained from the hospital. He chuckled at my persistence but said, "Look, I'm retired, I've got all the time in the world. If you want to waste a little of your own, come on over."

The next day, I showed him the hospital records. He reviewed them and shook his head, indicating that the records didn't help him remember. There was a picture of my client on the file from the time that he had treated her and he said, "So this is the patient, then." I confirmed that the photo had been taken around that time, but he said he still couldn't help me. When I got back to my office, the doctor had left a message for me to call him. When I did, the doctor asked me whether I could tell him if my client had ever complained about his treatment of her. I was somewhat embarrassed by the question, but I confirmed that my client had actually complained that he was very abrupt in his treatment of her and not very sensitive in his dealings with her at the time. He said, "Yes, yes, that's the woman, and you know what? I do remember that operation. When I removed the IUD, I clearly recall that the device had that distinctive crab shape of the Dalkon Shield."

Bingo! What delightful words to hear. And to think it was all a result of my client complaining about the doctor's treatment of her.

The moral of this story? Thoroughness is essential in representing clients. There were at least three points when I could have "accepted the inevitable" and given up on finding the proof. By persisting, I managed to earn a good settlement for my client—and her gratitude.

whether this is a first or follow-up interview. The point I would stress here is that, as with all aspects of interviewing, you are a professional who makes conscious choices at every stage in the process. In the perfect interviewing world, nothing is by chance.

THOROUGHNESS

When you work in a law office, you will encounter a constant source of reminders that thoroughness is essential to the work you do. A little oversight or sloppiness can be costly for the client and ultimately for the law firm. Attention to detail has won or lost more lawsuits than good intentions. Remember that the lawyer can be likened to a legal engine: it can only run well with a good supply of excellent fuel.

Working from a checklist can help you to obtain the information in a thorough manner. Checklists are good tools, but do not be a slave to them. If you follow a checklist lock-step, from beginning to end, you will almost certainly miss important information, perhaps even whole areas of information that were available from the client for the asking.

When asking questions, follow the flow of the answers. Satisfy yourself that you have gotten everything of value in a particular area before moving on. It helps to check with the client to see if she has anything further to add, before moving on to a new area of inquiry. Be open to the nuances of speech and body posture; they can help you to know whether the client is holding back on a thought, perhaps just waiting for a cue that it is all right to bring something up. Pace yourself—pause to consider how things are going, whether something feels like it is still hanging or incomplete. Take the time to do a complete interview; it may well be the best service you can provide a client.

> **"When asking questions, follow the flow of the answers. Satisfy yourself that you have gotten everything of value in a particular area before moving on."**

WINDING DOWN THE INTERVIEW

This is a very important stage in the interview process. An abrupt conclusion like, "Well, I think I have heard enough," leaves the client with a sense of incompleteness. It also has a quality of the schoolmaster dismissing the student from detention. A strange phenomenon happens in interviews: when the interviewer tells the client that the session is coming to a close, the client suddenly blurts out something of considerable importance. It is as if she has been saving the best for the last. More likely, the interview process has not touched on this point, and she has been waiting to reveal it.

Don't paint yourself into a corner on your allotment of time. If possible, let your client know at the beginning of the interview approximately how long the interview will take; this creates a subtle pressure on the client to bring up important issues before the interview draws to a close. In addition, if you keep the client informed about where you are in the interview ("We will now move on to discussion of your medical treatment") then the client can more easily determine where to "plug in" certain aspects of her information. Periodically asking the client if she has any questions or anything further to add is a good safeguard to avoid lost information.

"A strange phenomenon happens in interviews: when the interviewer tells the client that the session is coming to a close, the client suddenly blurts out something of considerable importance."

During the closing stage, several factors need attention. First, you may find it valuable to summarize what the client has told you, or, if you have done that throughout the interview, you could summarize the overall message. (Most summaries should be only a few sentences in length.) Second, you should always employ the "scoop question" toward the end of the interview. This can take many forms, but in essence you ask, "Is there anything else you can tell me that might be helpful?" Doing this after the summary has a way of focusing the client's attention on the important legal issues that you have identified in your summary. Third, you and the client should discuss the next step. ("We will prepare a draft will for you to review and comment on.") You should always review what the client has committed to doing, such as getting you the original of their marriage certificate or completing a financial statement—as well as what you will be doing, such as conducting a property search or sending a letter requesting documentation.

The client should usually leave your office with a list of tasks in her hand. And you may wish to remind your client, in a reporting letter, what she has agreed to do. This can also be filed as a memo, and it is a convenient way to confirm your understanding of what transpired, so you can invite the client to correct any errors. Finally, you should thank the client for helping you with this task. It is shameful flattery to tell the client that she has been a good interviewee, very clear and knowledgeable. Don't say this unless it has a ring of truth. However, positive statements, where they fit, leave the client "up" and optimistic about her legal representation.

Winding down an interview is an important process. Often, valuable information comes out at this stage or useful connections are made with the client. Frequently, students go through the motions of checking with the client to see if there is anything else that the client wishes to deal with; at the same time, these students send clear, non-verbal cues that the interview is over.

Most clients are very attuned, even hypersensitive to these non-verbal cues—the interviewer pushing away from the table, gathering up his papers, putting his pen away, looking at his watch, or other similar signals. Being polite Canadians, let alone clients who are somewhat uncertain with the process, their inclination is to think that the point they had wanted to bring up can wait; it is not important enough to keep you from your coffee break.

Your client might even dismiss a point she wanted to raise entirely, concluding that since you, the interviewer, didn't think anything more was required, nothing she could add would be helpful. After all, you're the expert. If you really want the client to search her mind to see if there is anything else she wants to add, make eye contact and consciously convey that there is all the time in the world and that you are truly interested in anything the client can contribute.

Is there anything else you can add to what you have told me? Anything at all, even if it seems insignificant to you, small items can be important.

YOUR INTERVIEWING STYLE

You will develop a style of interviewing whether you like it or not. The point of studying legal interviewing is so the style that you develop becomes a conscious choice rather than happenstance. Much of what you do in learning to interview, in improving your effectiveness as an interviewer, is to critique your own interviews, keeping an open mind as to how you can change and improve.

The interviews that you conduct are your laboratory, but if this process of learning is to be effective, you must find out how you can experience the interview process from outside your own perspective. One way of doing this is to have the interviews you do observed and critiqued by others. Another way is to ask clients how they felt about the interview. Many businesses do quality-control sampling, to see if their message is getting across, if their service is up to scratch. If you are able to tape some interviews, video or audio, this may help, particularly in the early stages, to see yourself from a distance. Watching other people conduct interviews is also valuable: you can observe how others deal with the interview problems that you encounter. Steal whatever is good from these observations—imitation is the highest form of flattery.

Your style of interviewing is personal to you and can be made very effective. Some tactics are more likely to get you into problems, and you'll find a few cautions listed in appendix E, "Inventory of Interviewing Inhibitors." Have a look at that and see how you can incorporate the do's and don'ts from the list into your interviewing forays.

Each time that you are able to observe yourself, choose a particular aspect of interviewing to observe: non-verbal behaviour, empathy, use of language. Look for verbal punctuation, like *uhms* and *ahs*; the repeated use of a pet word, like *right* or *OK*. All forms of verbal punctuation are acceptable in limited use, but they become irritating if used constantly. The client will find herself waiting for you to *righty-o* one more time as she tries to stop herself from screaming. Be aware that these habits may distract the client from her focus on the task at hand.

You must be open to criticism; it is the most valuable source of improvement you can have. At the same time, you must not become so sensitive to criticism that you become immobilized. Listen to suggestions and then let them slide into your subconscious as reminders.

> **"You must be open to criticism; it is the most valuable source of improvement you can have."**

CHAPTER QUESTIONS

True or false?

1. It is not very important for the client to get your name correctly, after all the lawyer is the person handling the file.   _____

2. Narrow questions are the most effective way to get a client's story out.   _____

3. You don't have to worry about the accuracy or detail of information you obtain, because there is plenty of time to work that out as the file progresses.   _____

4. The non-directive style of interviewing is the only correct way of conducting an interview.   _____

CHAPTER EXERCISES

Listen to or watch an interview. This can be in any context; it does not need to be in a legal setting.

1. Consider the ways in which the interviewer's style of fact-gathering influences the content of the interview.

2. What information would you have liked to have had from the interview that was "left on the table" at the end?

3. How could the interviewer have obtained a more complete picture in this interviewing situation?

CHAPTER 4

Environment of the Interview

In Brief

This chapter explores the importance of the environment that sets the stage of the interview. Some practical suggestions about how the environment can be improved are put forward.

Interviews can be conducted in many different locations and under a wide variety of conditions. A war correspondent may conduct an interview, with shells exploding and tracer bullets lighting the sky. A loan application interview may be conducted in a tiny cubicle, with adjacent employees able to hear all about the customer's private financial circumstances. A television host may conduct a "cozy" fireside interview in front of a million viewers.

You will conduct interviews in less-than-perfect surroundings. What you make of these limitations will depend on your personality and how you wish to come across.

The only mistake is to think that the physical surroundings don't matter. I rarely conduct interviews in my office. It has a window that looks onto an area frequently populated by young women who are invariably wearing mini dresses. There is also a large and cluttered desk between me and my clients.

Clutter can be very distracting, particularly when a client finds himself trying to read upside-down documents pertaining to another case. It is *not* the client's duty to avoid being "nosey"; it is up to the law firm to protect confidentiality. A file tag that says "Sarah Bloor—Matrimonial" tells any client that you are representing Ms. Bloor regarding a matrimonial matter. In a big city, this may not seem significant, but if your new client is Ms. Bloor's husband's old buddy, and the unfortunate Mr. Bloor is under the impression that his marriage is ticking along just fine, this could provide a significant problem for your firm.

In addition to protecting confidentiality, many people view clutter as wholly unprofessional. So, to avoid that whole issue, find a tidy, neutral interview space. Look at your office or selected interview space through the eyes of a stranger, someone seeing it for the first time. You may be shocked by what you see.

It is all about choices and personal style—not just your style, but a style that, hopefully, suits your client. You have to find the style that produces the best results. Does your client feel more important by sitting at an enormous and expensive table, the making of which helped to deplete the vanishing rainforest? Do you want to sit in a boardroom, giving your client the impressive view of the harbour and mountains beyond? Or do you want to sit kitty-corner to your client in a relatively intimate room that generates an atmosphere of a team focusing on the task at hand?

No one style suits every interviewer and no one style suits every client.

PHYSICAL SPACE

Before the interview, think about your client and the purpose of this particular interview. The following aspects of the environment are worth considering and, to the extent that you can, worth modifying to suit the interview you are about to conduct.

Room Size

Intimate or expansive? One client or many? If you have a choice between a small or large room, find out how many clients you are accommodating and, to the best of your ability, think of what will make them most comfortable. Don't grab the big boardroom because you like it or because it will enhance your status; use it if it will work best with this client (e.g., he is suing the owner of a high-rise because he's claustrophobic and he was trapped in an elevator). Also consider where the room is located relative to the reception area. Think about an older person or someone who has just had hip-replacement surgery.

Keep in mind that although "size counts," size isn't everything. A small room may be intimate, but a small room coldly furnished is unlikely to have the desired effect. A student once described an interview with an insurance adjuster where she was deposited in a small cubicle with cement walls. She described the room as feeling damp and cold. There were some posters, but they featured gruesome, automobile accidents—and one very prominently displayed poster discouraged insurance fraud.

It is quite possible that the insurance company's interviewers intended to make clients nervous and uncomfortable. The point? Small and intimate are not necessarily synonymous.

Colours

You can't repaint the office for each new client, but consider the impact of the room's colour scheme. My office has a sky blue ceiling with clouds painted on it. I like it. I am in the office a lot, so that is important. It also provides a "topic" for new clients to comment on—a fairly effective ice breaker—and it is quite relaxing for people who are in stressful situations, which is typical of most clients. However, some people have said that it looks like a daycare centre. Some lawyers would not like to project this image.

Furniture

If you don't think furniture is important, you may be too young to remember the *months* of wrangling to determine the shape of the table at the Paris peace talks, to end the Vietnam War. There are choices to be made. Table, desk, or only chairs? Along with the furniture, you must think about how you wish to arrange the seating. For each of the set-ups shown in the accompanying illustration (figure 4.1), decide the virtues and drawbacks. In choosing the furniture in your interview space, try to make it comfortable for both you and your client.

Distractions

Law offices are busy spaces, and it is your job to find an oasis of tranquility for your interview. This means no interruptions, no background music, no angry, tearful, loud, or otherwise distracting activities within your auditory or visual space. If your client notices that you ask your receptionist to hold your calls, it makes him feel important and valued, that your time with

"If your client notices that you ask your receptionist to hold your calls, it makes him feel important and valued, that your time with him is your top priority."

Figure 4.1   Interview Seating Arrangements

him is your top priority. Every person wants to think that he is the most important client you have, or at least too important to be displaced by some other "really important" matter. Some clients will act as if they are your only concern. The unspoken rule is not to disabuse them of this notion, except when it becomes necessary for the file lawyer to point out the monetary cost of the exclusive attention that they demand. This can work wonders in limiting a client's demanding nature.

> **"Every person wants to think that he is the most important client you have, or at least too important to be displaced by some 'really important' matter."**

INTERVIEW SPACES ELSEWHERE

It is not always possible—and sometimes not preferable—to conduct the interview at the law firm's offices. Some clients have great difficulty getting around; to accommodate their physical disability (whether temporary or permanent) it may be necessary to conduct the interview at the client's home or elsewhere, such as a hospital. I have conducted personal injury interviews in hospital rooms as well as taking instructions and attending for signing of wills in intensive-care wards. Naturally there are unique considerations that must not be forgotten, such as counsel satisfying herself that the client has the mental capacity to give instructions and to draft a will.

Frequently, hospital patients are given medication for pain or other purposes that can affect their ability to concentrate or understand elements of what you are discussing. Since a patient's condition may change radically from day to day, sufficient small talk, to satisfy oneself of the patient's condition, is important. Here's an example. A client who was in hospital (terminal cancer) wanted to finalize and sign his will. Before discussing the will, I talked with him about an upcoming election. He demonstrated an astute political analysis and lucidity of thought that would put my insights to shame. This conversation had the value of permitting me, if questioned about his capacity, to provide a specific example of why I believed he had capacity to sign the will. Wherever possible, we should attempt to save clients, particularly vulnerable clients, from those sorts of worries.

If you find yourself in such a situation, make some notes about the basis for your conclusions regarding the client's capacity. They will be very helpful if the matter is ever contested. Written notes at the time—when you are focused on the issue of capacity—will be powerful evidence. They also help to see that your client's last wishes are complied with.

INTERNAL DISTRACTORS

We all cart around internal distractors. Some of these are due to our multiple roles in life: interviewer, employee, parent, husband or wife, son or daughter. In a perfect world, the different roles stay in their place and allow you to function effectively in each separate role. Alas, it's not always a perfect world.

When one role is worrisome—your daughter's new boyfriend drives a motorcycle, your mother is ill—or just the business of living becomes overwhelming, these can cause you to steal time from the client, by not giving him your full attention. Maybe you are just making a mental shopping list, because you have to rush home to make supper; regardless of what your preoccupation is, the client receives less than full attention. If you find yourself doing this, you should realize that you are not practising active listening but have become a passive participant in the interview. You might just as well have turned on the tape machine and left the room. The withdrawal of your energy from the interview will obviously affect the quality of information you receive. You need to find ways of refocusing yourself and adding vigour to your participation in the interview process.

What if you don't like the client? What if he puts you off with his mannerisms and personality? the way he dresses? his hairstyle or personal grooming? A negative reaction to your client may be based on his age, race, religion, or sexual orientation.

I assume that, in today's world, I needn't comment on the inappropriateness of such biases. However, prejudice continues to exist, a hold-over from a less-tolerant, more-bigoted era. Ignoring the prejudice does not make it disappear, but if you acknowledge it, you may resist its pernicious influence. And where you aren't able to eradicate your prejudices, you must minimize or eliminate their impact on your interviewing.

> **"You need to find ways of refocusing yourself and adding vigour to your participation in the interview process."**

EMOTIONAL ENVIRONMENT

Although the physical environment is important, its significance is found in the impact it has on the emotional environment of the interview. The client's comfort, level of trust, and ability to confide in you can be affected by the environment that you create.

Your non-verbal communication with the client also helps to establish the emotional environment of the interview. You may locate the interview in an intimate space, but if you cringe away from the client, this will not enhance the emotional environment of the interview.

Another factor in the emotional environment is the client's non-verbal signals. They can tell you some things about his emotional state. If your client is leaning forward and making good eye contact, then he is likely feeling good about the interview, involved and actively participating. If he is leaning away, avoiding eye contact, or huffing at your comments or questions, then it may be time to try a new tack or try to determine what is impeding his full involvement in the interview.

The purpose of structuring the physical environment is to help your client open up and work with the firm to explore ways to overcome the legal concerns that caused him to seek professional help.

MENTAL VACATIONS

Just as you will have internal distractors, clients too are subject to the same influences. Since the client is usually responding to your questions, your focus can help keep him on track. However, from time to time, you need to impart information to the client, and if the client's mind is wandering while you are "imparting"—no matter how well you state the information—it will be lost somewhere in the client's misty subconscious.

It will not always be obvious when a client is not following your comments; we have all learned to mask our wandering minds. You may be adept at spotting the

I once worked in an after-hours, emergency social services office. Some staff members provided emergency shelter and meal tickets for adult "street" people. The interviewing space was a little cubicle where the financial-assistance worker sat opposite the client, across a small desk with a computer. A consistent issue these interviewers had was the stench that emanated from some of the clients, many of whom had been living and sleeping on the street, often for years. Their body odour was overwhelmingly offensive. Most of the workers did not blame the individual, but it nevertheless made their job very difficult. At times, workers could not complete their task without moving away from the individual, the smell was so strong.

To deal with this issue, most workers found some way to mask the smell without further demeaning the client. One worker installed her own ionizing air cleaner on the desk; another liberally applied perfume; and yet another held an orange near her nose, as if she was about to eat it. These tactics were, perhaps, not too subtle, but at least these efforts did not subject the clients to additional emotional trauma.

Stone walls do not a prison make,
Nor iron bars a cage;
Minds innocent and quiet take
That for an hermitage;
If I have freedom in my love
And in my soul am free,
Angels alone, that soar above,
Enjoy such liberty.

— *Richard Lovelace,*
"To Althea, from Prison"

wandering mind. If so, try some subtle actions to bring the person back to the topic at hand.

Do you have any questions about that?
(Pause for answer)

Would you like me to repeat that for you?

Would you like to write that down?

Depending on how comfortable you feel with the client, you may choose to take a not-so-subtle approach.

I notice that you appear to be distracted.
Would you like to take a break?

Knock, knock, is anybody home?

I suspect that I may be boring you. Would it
be better if I put some of this in writing? or if
we dealt with it another day?

If you use this approach, be sure that you know the client well. Being sensitive to the client's ability to focus on the information you require can be very helpful. In many instances, when dealing with clients who have had head injuries, I have had to take interviews in small steps, with numerous breaks between sessions. Often, the client who has a reduced capacity to function mentally is not aware of his own limitations. He continues to think of himself as having a "mind like a steel trap," because that is how he was in his heyday. It may be necessary to step lightly around this issue. It is not helpful to tell the client, "You're making no sense at all." A better way would be to ask the client if he would mind if you took a brief break, so you could get a drink of water. And you could invite the client to walk around or have a coffee in the interim.

Whatever approach you take, pretending that the client is "with you," when he clearly is not, is useless. If you ignore this problem, you will never know how much of the information, which you were trying to impart, was missed. You will always be subject, at some point in the future, to the client complaining, "Why didn't you tell me that before?"

CHAPTER QUESTIONS

1. Outline three components of the physical environment for an interview that you have control over.

2. In the office set-ups pictured in figure 4.1, consider what message is being conveyed with each arrangement.

CHAPTER EXERCISE

The next time you are the "subject" of an interview, think about the physical space. What does the environment do to your mood, your openness, your comfort with the process? Consider ways in which the environment could be improved to assist in gathering the information the interviewer seeks.

CHAPTER 5

The Interview

In Brief

This chapter examines the various components of an interview, starting with some of the mechanics of the process. Listening skills and the value of empathic communications are particularly emphasized.

NOTE TAKING

An interview can be very long and detailed. No one can be expected to preserve it entirely in his memory. As we have said, law offices run on detail, so the details must be accurately recorded. But how do you maintain eye contact with the client and still make notes that are legible for later action? Over the years, students have suggested that interviews can be tape-recorded. Even some interviewing texts offer this as an alternative.

Recording is usually not a good option, for a number of reasons. Requesting to do this in the preliminary interview will put off many people. Your client may feel pressured into agreeing, when she is not comfortable that a person she doesn't know will be recording intimate details of her life. She may also wonder whether you are recording the conversation because you don't trust her; after all, recordings are often used because of this. Even if the client happily agrees to be taped, you, the interviewer, have now doubled or tripled your workload: you have to review the tape later or even have the tape transcribed. This is a colossal waste of client funds and firm resources. Resist the temptation to record; concentrate on good note taking.

> **"You should always review your notes while the client is present, and often relate back to the client a summary of what she has told you."**

Where possible, your notes should reflect the client's own language. It is tempting to "translate" what the client has said into legal language. In doing so, you have done a disservice to your client. Don't put words in your client's mouth. Let her tell the story in a way that is as advantageous as possible, given the irrefutable facts. Because, if you get it "right" at the beginning, you have provided an invaluable service because this is the description that will be repeated throughout the pre-trial and trial process.

Much of what you record will be transferred to the lawyer, to assist him in shaping the legal issues. The more faithful your notes are to the client's words, the more the lawyer will be helped in his task.

Notes are also useful during the interview, not just afterward. You should always review your notes while the client is present, and often relate back to the client a summary of what she has told you. The client is then given a chance to correct mistakes and, as stated earlier, the sooner that happens the better. Most trial lawyers use notepads with a wide margin on the right-hand side (for right-handed lawyers). This allows him to record the witness's (client's) evidence in the main portion of the paper and to make parallel notations helpful for further questioning or cross-examination in the margin. In a client interview, when she provides some information that you wish to follow up on, a margin note of "more" or "ask" allows the client to continue with her story, uninterrupted, but ensures that when you review your notes, toward the end of the interview, this issue can then be re-examined.

Remember to maintain good eye contact during the interview. This does *not* mean regularly glancing up at the client, it means *real* eye contact, so that she knows you are following her story with interest. Although shorthand is a dying art, some form of speed writing is valuable in this process.

Ud b surprzd hw ez it is 2 devlp yr own spd rtng mthd.

Many books address this topic but, one way or another, you should devise some reliable shortcuts to help record client responses. Some interviewers effectively use a laptop computer. The machine can be alienating for some clients, but the screen can be set up so that only a slight shift of the eyes is needed to put the interviewer back in touch with his client. In addition, most legal professionals I know are faster, experience less strain, and are more accurate with a laptop than in writing. Laptops provide the additional advantage of easy cutting and pasting into other applications, such as affidavits or pleadings. If you use a laptop, be sure that your client is comfortable with that; remember, many people find law offices machine-like to start with. Part of our job is to ensure that our firms are approachable.

You may want to stop the client from time to time, to ensure that you have some particular information recorded correctly. I have never experienced a client who did not respect the need for precision in legal matters. You might say, "Excuse me, but you have made a very important point here. Let me be sure that I have gotten that down accurately." Reviewing information with the client to ensure accuracy is a valuable process. You will find it surprising how often this process results in an important correction—or in eliciting a valuable piece of information that the client recalls upon hearing her story replayed.

Oh, yeah, I almost forgot to tell you about the cocaine in the car.

OBSERVATION SKILLS

Keenness of observation means being able to "read" your client and provide appropriate reactions to her. As indicated elsewhere, both intentional and unintentional communication must be interpreted. To be a keen observer, you must be aware of the effect of your own behaviour on others. If you are a physically domineering person with a booming voice, you will be used to encountering people who appear shy or intimidated. In your everyday life, you may be comfortable with having this impact on other people, but you should not allow this domineering mode to govern your relations with your clients. You may have to make an extra effort to encourage their involvement, perhaps by softening your voice or using non-verbal techniques in drawing clients out about their legal concerns.

On the other hand, if you are diminutive and soft spoken, you may need to adopt more assertive poses in order to command a necessary level of respect from some clients. Confirming that you are a trained and qualified legal assistant or developing a firm handshake and an assertive tone may assist you in winning more attention.

Be aware of how your clients are reacting to you, so that you can adapt your style to suit their needs. You should also be aware of how your own perceptions or biases can affect your ability to observe. If you tend to believe that many young people are dishonest, sneaky, and selfish, then you might reconsider working with a lawyer whose primary practice is with young offenders. From time to time, you will almost certainly have to deal with people who make you uncomfortable. As a professional, you must set aside that discomfort and provide the best representation possible for these individuals. Law firms supply professional services to a wide range of customers. Biases distort our perception of the world.

If you have a bias about other races or groups, your expectations tend to be fulfilled—you see what you want to see.

Once you are aware of your biases you may be able to avoid the distortions they cause and create a more-objective interviewing experience.

> **"I have never experienced a client who did not respect the need for precision in legal matters."**

I recently spent two weeks building houses in Guatemala. I was reminded of the stereotype of the Latino worker, laying in the sun, with the attitude that *mañana* would suffice to get the work done. The local workers on the project started before 7 a.m., worked without break till lunchtime, and after half an hour continued their work, well past the time that the international volunteers went home. The local workers put in a twelve-hour-plus day, sometimes in intense heat. At times, trying to keep pace with their efforts, I wished that they would adopt the relaxed-worker stereotype.

NON-VERBAL COMMUNICATION

When you smash your thumb with a hammer, we can tell what you're feeling, even without the aid of the colourful language that is likely to follow. When you open that yoghurt container that got lost in the back of the fridge three months ago, your facial expression tells the story. If you are standing at the bus stop, and a gang of rowdy youths pulls up on their motorcycles, your body is likely to display a degree of tension. In all these scenarios, non-verbal communication is expected; any observer would recognize the sentiments being conveyed.

Non-verbal communication allows us to interpret the world around us. Curiously, most people are good at "reading" these signals but not as skilled at controlling or manipulating what they non-verbally communicate to others. That is because non-verbal communication is often unintended and, therefore, unregulated. For this reason, it is seen as more honest.

We recognize a person's mood or intentions from observing both subtle and not-so-subtle expressions, without any verbal content. Basic emotions are displayed through facial expressions, body posture, muscle tension, or other non-verbal clues.

As an interviewer, you need to hone your skills at reading these signals, to better understand what your client is communicating. Where appropriate, you should put this knowledge to use in your interactions with your client.

A client who seems anxious might be soothed with small talk and humour. If a client becomes tense around a particular topic, you might veer away from discussing this matter until later, or you might soften the experience, for the client, with various assurances. Remaining blissfully ignorant of the signals should not be an option. This would be like conducting the interview while playing loud rock music. Don't handicap yourself by ignoring signals that are there to detect. That's just counterproductive.

As an interviewer, you will also need to use non-verbal signals that are consonant with the words you are saying. It may be urban myth, but a story exists that McDonald's management trainees take a program that, among other things, teaches them to deal with subordinate employees. A supervisor, in dealing with a request from an employee to speak with her, should look at her watch in an obvious manner and say, "Of course I have time to speak with you." The not-so-subtle message is, make it quick; I am a busy person. In this example, the non-verbal communication is not consistent with what the supervisor actually says. Because telling an employee you don't have time for him is not acceptable, the supervisor (employer) uses communication that is clearly understood by the employee but nearly impossible to specify in a grievance. This is psychological intimidation.

> **"As an interviewer, you need to hone your skills at reading these signals, to better understand what your client is communicating."**

So, am I saying that you should manipulate the client with your non-verbal communication? Well, manipulation is a loaded word. Think of it as influencing. If you consciously lean forward, soften your voice, and make eye contact, you are trying to influence your client, by letting her know your concern. It is not for some devious, ulterior purpose—you aren't trying to sell her a used car. You are simply using a technique to improve the communication and working relationship between you and your client.

On the other hand, if your client is nervous and you are jiggling your foot under the desk and twirling your pen, you are not likely to help her relax.

> **"If you consciously lean forward, soften your voice, and make eye contact, you are trying to influence your client, by letting her know your concern."**

In watching a student interview recently, I observed a significant example of how non-verbal communication can be leading. The client had been on a cruise when a piece of a chandelier had broken off and landed on her head. The interviewer, wanting to know how big the piece of chandelier was, but being careful to choose words that would not lead the client, simply asked, "How big was the piece that struck you on the head?" The problem was that, while asking the question, the interviewer gestured with her hands as though she was holding an invisible cantaloupe. The gesture conveyed a very specific size and, although I am sure that the interviewer did not want to lead the client, it would not have surprised me if the client's response had conformed with the gestured size. Particularly significant is that neither the interviewer nor the client would realize the subtle persuasion taking place and that the actual facts may well be misstated.

In addition to communicating meaning through your facial expression and posture, you convey messages by the way you situate yourself in relation to others. This is sometimes termed proxemics. To illustrate: we tend to stand closer to people we like; we tend to directly face people we are attracted to, and we turn away from those to whom we are not attracted.

Even with friends, we alter our body positions, depending on our mood. Spatial considerations are also linked to culture and ethnicity: personal space differs not only among individuals but also between people of different cultures. In some "Latin" cultures, speakers stand almost on each others toes and appear most comfortable speaking while touching the listener or gently holding his arm—and the force of the speaker's grip will change with how animated their conversation is, and with how important or upsetting the discussion is to them.

In an interview, one effective, non-verbal technique is to *not* ask a question. The use of pauses and the basic cadence of the questioning can have a significant impact on the progress and success of an interview. The next time you are involved in an interview—or even a conversation—try silence. You ask something, your significant other responds, and you simply wait … and wait … and wait.

It is surprising how unsettling a five-second pause can be, let alone ten or fifteen seconds. You may discover some surprising things about your friends or spouse that you would never have known if you "forged on" with the next comment. This is not to say that you should play "head games" with your friends, spouse, or clients for that matter; but a little experimenting with short but significant pauses might produce valuable information that would otherwise be lost—well worth the fleeting discomfort that may arise.

What about the interviewer's voice inflection? The same content delivered with an emphasis on a different word—or using a different tone of voice—can communicate a very different message. Look at the question below and the variations in emphasis, and see if you agree with the interpretations.

> *What is your problem?*
>
> A simple indication of curiosity or an offer to assist in solving a difficulty.
>
> **What** *is your problem?*
>
> Bewilderment, an indication that the speaker is annoyed and exasperated?
>
> *What* **is** *your problem?*
>
> I don't understand it. You need to explain it.

*What is **your** problem?*

It's not my problem, it's your problem—don't bother me with it.

*What is your **problem**?*

I can't understand why this is a problem for you. A normal person wouldn't have a problem with this.

"Of course, you could be repeatedly making the same mistake unless you find opportunities to check your interpretations."

The science-fiction book *Dune* has a scene in which the visitor is meeting Duke Atriedes for the first time, and the visitor spits on the table at the end of the meeting. Coming from a desert planet, this expenditure of the most precious resource is considered a tribute to the host. Fortunately, the host has been well coached and restrains his lieutenants from killing the visitor. From their perspective, the duke's protectors saw this as an insult, perhaps a threat to the duke's safety. The visitor was offering the greatest compliment he could make.

It is possible to misinterpret nervousness as evasiveness, anxiety as hostility. There is no guaranteed method for interpreting non-verbal signals with certainty. Practice is good and applying yourself to learning this skill is important. Of course, you could be repeatedly making the same mistake unless you find opportunities to check your interpretations. You cannot always do this when interviewing clients, but you may be able to use your long-suffering friends as guinea pigs in your quest for knowledge.

All of the above variations in the question could take on wholly different meanings when delivered in different tones of voice, at different paces, with different facial expressions, in varying proximity to the listener, with different postures or gestures.

When interpreting non-verbal signals, you should try to rise above your own personal perspective, not to be influenced by personal beliefs that might affect your perceptions. Remember that one gesture can be interpreted differently by people. Each person has his or her own perspective.

I noticed that when I asked you to take out the garbage you exhaled and rolled your eyes. What were you communicating with those gestures?

You may be able to check on some non-verbal signals with clients, without alienating them, and eliminate the possibility of erroneous interpretations.

You appear to be uncomfortable talking about this right now. Am I reading you right?

Well, a little bit, I guess.

What is it that makes you uncomfortable?

Well, it's kind of embarrassing admitting I was taken for a fool.

Oh, I see. Well, it never occurred to me that you would feel that way. These sorts of things happen often. After all, you were simply trusting another person.

Ya ... I guess, well, what do you need to know?

It is far better that your interpretations be "on the table" than misunderstood and lead to inaccuracies. Of course, not all non-verbal messages can, or need to be, verbalized, some are best left unspoken. However, where you can check your interpretation without offending your client, it may assist in clearing the air and help you to refine your abilities.

So, as an interviewer, you want to become adept at reading non-verbal signals and equally adept at conveying meaning non-verbally. This is not a psychological game but an important mode of communication. To deny the existence or impact of such communication would be like wearing a cowboy hat wrapped in plastic. You're going to look like an idiot, whether you acknowledge it or not.

THE ART OF LISTENING

We have all been in that embarrassing situation where someone has been talking for quite a while, but you have not been really *listening*. Someone interrupts, and then the speaker says, "Now, where was I?" You really don't want to say, "I have no idea at all," or "How should I know? I haven't taken in a word you've said in the last half hour."

You certainly don't want to say this if the speaker is someone with any measure or authority or control over your life, like a teacher or boss. So your mind frantically searches for an answer. It's embarrassing, and it's not likely to get you votes in the good-listener category.

Although some of us have a reasonably good auditory memory, even on autopilot, "faking it" won't get you far with real-life clients. They require far too much attention to let you get by with phony attention. When interviewing, particularly a new client, you should be in high observation mode, attending to verbal and non-verbal signals, being sensitive to voice modulations and any indications of stress, and being alert to signals that suggest a contradiction between the words said and the non-verbal language.

Why are some people good listeners? Here are a few attributes. A *good listener* is someone who:

1. pays attention to what you are saying;

2. appears interested in what you are saying, interested in you as a person;

3. lets you know verbally or non-verbally that they are still "with you";

4. helps to frame your thoughts, to play back what you are saying;

At the airport recently, I saw a man who I assumed was returning from a vacation. For the most part, he looked pretty cool—he was tanned and well groomed and he wore a discreet earring. He also wore a cowboy hat—a style choice that I can respect. This hat, however, was wrapped in plastic.

During the half hour that I walked through the airport, I must have seen him 10 times. Everywhere I went, there was this otherwise good-looking person wearing a cowboy hat wrapped in plastic. He was oblivious to how ridiculous he looked and the impact that his attire had on others.

What lesson is there in this for interviewers? Well, first, don't conduct your interviews wearing a cowboy hat wrapped in plastic. Second, be aware that you communicate, intentionally or not, through your actions as much as your words.

On the television show *20/20*, Mike Wallace was interviewing a man who was in the people-persuasion business. He sold a service through infomercials. He talked about the art of mimicking as a subtle form of persuasion. What he was referring to was the process where the seller copies the non-verbal posture of the person he wants to influence. The theory is that this person finds himself subtly influenced by the speaker, trusting him and confident in his abilities, because it is like looking in a mirror. You see familiar behaviour and feel an empathic bond with the speaker. During this interview, the salesman began to put what he was preaching into practice. He would stroke his chin a few seconds after Mike Wallace did, and cross his legs or lean forward, subtly copying Mike Wallace's gestures. It was interesting to watch Mr. Wallace's reaction: his attention was held by the speaker, he nodded appreciatively at points made by him. At one point, he even said that he did feel attracted to the salesman. And I'm almost certain that Wallace was unaware that the very technique being described was being employed on him.

5. can summarize your point or even take it one step further;

6. lets you get your point out without cutting you off;

7. ignores distractions; and

8. is responsive to the content and emotion in your statements.

You probably can name more attributes, but what you need to ask yourself, honestly, is whether you would be seen as a good listener. Try to separate your personal life from your professional life; they may be (should be) different.

Listening to the client requires that you allow her to tell her story, without interruption. The client should never feel that she is competing with you for air space. If you suddenly find yourself talking at the same time as the client, you should apologize and shut up. You must remember whose content is important, and it is a major part of your job to encourage your client to provide complete information, not just the highlights.

"Listening to the client requires that you allow her to tell her story, without interruption."

There is more to it than simply being a good listener. The interview process requires that you also communicate to the client that you have heard and understood her. This process spans the range of nodding and vocal affirmations to summarizing what she has told you. You do this to ensure that you have gotten all the content that she wished to communicate, and gotten it correctly. This reassures your client, and it is a valuable way to assure accuracy. Telling the client what you are doing is part of this strategy.

I would now like to summarize what you have told me. I want to be sure that I have clearly understood your situation. Please listen with a critical ear and tell me where I may have misunderstood what you have told me. It's important that we have things right, from the beginning.

By approaching matters like this, you show the client that you have a system and that you are taking care to ensure accuracy. Some people summarize frequently, as they go through an interview; others only do it when they feel there is a likelihood of misunderstanding. The danger in the latter approach is that you may think you have it right when you don't. So, at the very least, summarize the key points for the client.

"Just nodding your head is a form of encouragement and can be very useful in greasing the communication wheels."

Just nodding your head is a form of encouragement and can be very useful in greasing the communication wheels. People like to know you are "with them," that you haven't gone off to dreamland. An intervention can serve more than one purpose. You can let the client know you are following her story as well as communicate other important information. Perhaps you could say,

"That's very helpful. Could you elaborate on this?" or *"What an astute observation. Would you tell me more?"*

Stroking a client's ego a bit not only encourages her to continue supplying you with valuable information, it gives her a positive feeling about her dealings with the law firm. A comment like, "That must have been terribly embarrassing when you fell down the steps," acknowledges the emotional content of what she has told you—a good approach to establishing client rapport and showing empathy—as well as checking that you have, indeed, captured the essence of what she has just told you. A direct comment like, "Now, am I right in concluding that you burned all of your husband's clothing?" tells the client you are following the story and checking pertinent facts.

From a kind of values-clarification perspective, you can ask a client, "How did you feel about firing your ex-husband's best friend?" This probes for more information; at the same time, it causes the client to reflect on her behaviour, something that may be helpful later.

The main point here is not just to listen well but to listen with a purpose. That purpose is always to advance the interests of the client by obtaining the most complete information, focusing the inquiry on relevant areas, and ensuring that the client feels valued and included in the process.

While you are listening to the client, you must not just blindly record everything she says. You must also evaluate the contents to determine its reliability. It is important here to distinguish between credibility and reliability. Credibility involves the speaker's intention—is she attempting to deceive you?—whereas reliability is independent of intention. Reliability is about assessing the value of the information. Let's say, for example, that a witness tells you that she got a good look at the robber as he ran under the streetlight after knocking the complainant to the ground. A visit to the scene reveals that there is no street lighting where the incident occurred, that the witness was 50 feet away, and a bus shelter blocks the view from the witness's vantage point. The witness may be trying to be helpful, may even think she saw what she claims to have seen, but the information is not reliable.

> "The purpose of good listening is always to advance the interests of the client by obtaining the most complete information, focusing the inquiry on relevant areas, and ensuring that the client feels valued and included in the process."

This is not to suggest that you cross-examine clients to try to expose the flaws in their description of events, but it is essential that you listen with a critical ear, so that you can question apparent inconsistencies. It is equally important that, if you notice contradictions and inconsistencies, you bring these to the attention of the lawyer who is handling the matter. Remember, no surprises make for happier lawyers.

Fascinating research has been done on eyewitness identification by Elizabeth F. Loftus at the University of Washington. She has found that eyewitness testimony is influenced by so many factors that its reliability must be seriously questioned in court.

> To name just a few [factors]: what questions witnesses are asked by police and how the questions are phrased; the difficulty people have in distinguishing among people of other races; whether witnesses have seen photos of suspects before viewing the lineup from which they pick out the person they say committed the crime; the size, composition and type (live or photo) of the lineup itself.*

* Elizabeth F. Loftus, "Eyewitness: Essential but Unreliable" (February 1984) *Psychology Today*.

Dr. Loftus points out that the perceptions of violent events, contrary to common beliefs, are less reliable, that stress clouds our perceptions. Victims tend to overstate the length of time a violent crime takes, and there is little or no relationship between witnesses' confidence in their ability to identify an accused and their actual ability to do so.

Therefore, in questioning a client, don't just ask whether she got a good look at the other person, ask questions that will aid in determining the objective ability of the client to observe what she claims to have seen.

You say you got a good look at the person with the weapon. I want to make sure that I have a clear, visual understanding of the scene. Where were you standing?

By the pickup truck.

What time of day was it?

About 11 p.m.

Can you describe any lighting that existed at the scene?

Well, it was a cloudy night, but there was still some light cast by the burning cross on Harvey's front lawn.

And how far was that from where the confrontation took place?

About 200 feet.

Where was the cross in relation to the confrontation?

Behind the people who were fighting.

I want you to visualize the scene. Could you see anyone's facial features?

Well, no. The light was behind them, their faces were all in shadow.

Finding a contradiction in the client's statements need not lead to confrontation. But if you ignore the contradiction, you will miss valuable information. It is far better that these matters are resolved in the interview than to have them discredit your client when they come out in cross-examination.

Some authors even suggest re-enactments to aid the client in remembering a particular event. This may be of assistance, but would be time-consuming and therefore expensive to arrange, and the same applies to visiting the scene of the event or accident. This can be helpful but not cost-effective. In most instances, the process of visualization with pointed questions is enough to assure the reliability of the information. Where the client has the opportunity to examine photographs, this may add to what she can tell you.

Wherever possible, make use of diagrams, preferably created by the client. These can be excellent sources of information. Make sure that you have pen and paper available for the client. In some circumstances, such a document can even become evidence in a proceeding. Be sure to "work" the diagram, don't just have a client draw it out and then put it in the file. In your interview, review the diagram to be sure you understand everything depicted in it. Label or have the client label important points. The client can include estimates of sizes and distances, can comment on colours, or indicate obstacles to a clear view. Any of these might not be apparent if you don't ask the questions.

Diagrams can be a helpful focus for the interview—and a tangible product of your joint efforts. People will vary in their skill levels, but rarely will a diagram not assist in providing a new and valuable perspective on a situation.

HOW TO LISTEN

In dyadic (two-way) communication, there are basically two components: talking and listening. These components are interrelated: listening helps the talking be more effective; talking helps listening be more effective. One way of analyzing the listening process is to break it up into passive listening and active listening.

> **"Diagrams can be a helpful focus for the interview—and a tangible product of your joint efforts."**

Passive Listening

The most passive form of listening is simply being unresponsive. Children use this technique to goad their parents. It drives adults crazy. In an interview, unresponsive behaviour is frustrating; however, silence is not always unresponsive. Silence can be used to encourage speaking, and it can be very effective because few people are comfortable with silence in a social setting. But most people need some time to reflect, to consider their words. Often, when a person pauses, we "helpfully" fill in the word for them.

> **"Often, when a person pauses, we 'helpfully' fill in the word for them."**

If we do this more than once, the speaker may become resigned to your choice for her words, and she may not correct misinterpretations; she will just let you make whatever assumptions you wish, right or wrong. The only way to know, absolutely, what a person would have said is to let her say it. Just wait until she finds the word she is searching for. Don't look bored. Don't display irritation. Just calmly let her gather her thoughts. Usually, it's a worthwhile wait.

Silence can also be used when the speaker has finished her comment. The ball is in your court, but if you respond, the other person will often fill the silence. This technique can be used when the speaker is being superficial or even evasive. Police officers make use of this in interrogations. Of course, your clients should not be "interrogated," but a measure of silence can be very effective in drawing out shy, uncertain, even evasive people. Experiment with silence. It can be a powerful tool if used in a conscious and genuine way.

The car that hit us was red.

[*Silence.*]

Actually kind of a maroon colour.

[*Silence.*]

With a white top.

[*Silence.*]

And a broken tail light.

[*Silence.*]

The first three letters on the licence plate were LDK.

[*Silence.*]

And one hubcap came off at the scene.

[*Pause*] *… Was there anything else you noticed about the car?*

A more moderate form of passive listening incorporates gestures such as nods, smiles, and neutral body language. A step up from this involves minimal verbal communication such as *hmmm, oh,* or a few encouraging words. To be useful, these interjections must be reasonably timed, encouraging, and non-judgmental. Even a minimalist comment like, "Oh, really" or "hmmm" could put the freeze on an interview if it is seen as a criticism. For example:

Sandy: I've decided to drop out of school.

Mother: Oh, really.

Sandy: Ya, well … it doesn't do any good anyway.

Mother: Hmmm.

Sandy: Why are you always judging me?

"Mother" has not said anything overtly critical, but "Sandy," partly because of family history, hears criticism.

We all know the value of the good listener—someone who is attentive and encouraging, even with only smiles, nods, or verbal encouragement. "Isn't that nice." "Wow." "Tell me more." "Fascinating." A good listener is adept at this, and the words tend to flow from the speaker like a bubbling brook.

Like service from a good waiter, the key is timing; too much is intrusive; just enough is encouraging. With effective passive listening, the listener is not out of the conversation; both parties are very much engaged in it. With acknowledgments that are noncommittal, the speaker can continue to direct the conversation where she chooses, but the speaker always knows her input is valued and desired.

Open-ended questioning, discussed in the next chapter, is another technique that is relatively passive, because it allows the speaker to choose the content of her answer, while the questioner directs the topics to be covered.

Active Listening

Most people listen actively, almost instinctively, or we learn this skill from an early age. So, if most of us know it, why do we study active listening? The answer: a casual conversation and a legal interview are quite different, and the result of missed communications or misunderstandings in the legal context can be disastrous. As professionals, we must use our skills to obtain the best results for the client—from the initial contact, through various information gathering exercises, to the (hopefully successful) outcome.

Remember that passive listening essentially involves being there for the client to talk to. However, friends, family members, and politicians often use aggressive conversational techniques. Think of conversations where the other person is talking while you are talking, raising his voice to be heard above your comments—or to drown out your comments—or simply waiting for you to take a breath before he barges in. Some accomplished speakers have learned the subtle art of breathing through their noses while speaking, so that the flow of air is continuous, as is their speech. No break in the flow of conversation—no opportunity for we polite Canadians to break in with a word or two.

Can you call it a conversation when each of the two people anxiously wait for an opportunity to break in with a continuation of his or her stream of consciousness—interjections, opinions, observations, remarks that seem to have no connection with the other speaker's comments? Aggressive conversation, however, is not a technique for interviewing clients. If you want information from clients, you need to listen.

Your repertoire of responses should move comfortably from the passive to the active, on a continuum, attempting to direct your replies to the needs of the client. Somewhat more active, then, are minimally intrusive responses: the nodding of the head, the *mm-hmm, is that so? really? yes?* These responses should be noncommittal, without value judgment. They can be effective in encouraging the client to continue her narrative. Even these responses *can* be problematic if spoken with a judgmental tone.

> So, I guess ... well, I had a few too many drinks.
>
> *Oh, really?*
>
> Well, yes, and I guess I shouldn't have tried to drive home.
>
> *Right.*
>
> And, I probably took the turn too fast.
>
> *That's for sure.*

If you think you are being careful with your words, and you still detect resistance, then nine times out of ten it's your tone that sunk you.

While your responses may be minimal, a client who is already feeling guilty or stupid will be very sensitive to your reactions and will often search for hidden meaning.

More-active responses—along the continuum—are comments that draw the client out but do not, in themselves, indicate a value judgment or clue as to the "right" answer.

> I guess I had too much to drink.
>
> *Can you tell me how much alcohol you consumed?*
>
> I must have been speeding.
>
> *What speed were you going, just prior to the collision?*

"The technique of active listening involves both listening to the client (to be sure you understand what she has said) and communicating to the client your understanding (to assure her that you appreciate both the content and emotion surrounding her comments)."

I guess she was right to be mad at me.

And why do you feel that?

On the most-active end of the spectrum, you, the interviewer, become more involved in trying to draw out the client's meaning. But be careful not take over the conversation. After all, what you are trying to do is obtain accurate information, not put words in the client's mouth.

The technique of active listening involves both listening to the client (to be sure you understand what she has said) and communicating to the client your understanding (to assure her that you appreciate both the content and emotion surrounding her comments). And these "active" comments should also be non-judgmental.

If you do not communicate your appreciation of the emotional content of your clients' responses, they will often "stew" over this, wondering whether you really understand their concerns, whether you have the whole picture. For the client, the emotional component is often 80 percent of her motivation to come to your office. You can have all the "facts" down cold, but without the emotional understanding she is left with a "cold" feeling about the law firm's ability to help her.

Some authorities suggest that the interviewer label what the client is feeling, to communicate his understanding of this. This is a tricky area since, by labelling, you can *mislabel* and take the interview onto a confusing detour.

I feel anxious about dealing with this separation agreement with my husband.

So you feel physically threatened about his response to being served with the papers.

By moving the conversation into this area, a whole set of procedures are likely to be put into place, including *ex parte*, no-contact orders that are likely to cause unpleasantness and difficulty in resolving the proceedings. Litigation rather than negotiated settlement becomes more likely. This may be good for business, but it is definitely bad for clients. Perhaps a better approach would be:

I feel anxious about dealing with this separation agreement with my husband.

That's understandable. What exactly is it that concerns you about the separation?

This focuses the client's comments and thoughts, without pushing her in a particular direction. Perhaps your client is anxious about financial concerns or whether her spouse will take his share of child-caring responsibilities. Regardless of what it is, without getting this information from the client, her needs cannot be addressed.

A concern or a strong emotion that is expressed by the client should be dealt with. Otherwise, it could fester and resurface later, allowing little or nothing to be accomplished while the client "stews" over the issue. Do not let this happen.

Sometimes the client will make inappropriate comments. These are even more difficult to deal with. However, they need to be acknowledged and addressed, or else they will harm the atmosphere of the interviews, sometimes irretrievably.

That bastard has got to pay for sleeping around on me.

Now, Mrs. Jones, I can appreciate that this is a very difficult time for you, but we need to focus on the legal issues facing you. Using that language makes me uncomfortable, and it makes it more difficult for us to work on the best solution to your concerns.

Do not ignore—let alone encourage—this style of talk or behaviour. If you spend the afternoon trashing her former loved one, there will be little to show for it, and the next meeting will be filled with expletives as the client tries to test the limits of decorum in the law office. Better to deal with sexist, racist, religious, homophobic slurs immediately and effectively. *Nip it in the bud.*

While client concerns should be dealt with as they arise, sometimes a client's issues are not verbalized. But non-verbal clues to underlying emotional concerns should also be addressed where possible. Jiggling of the foot or drumming of the fingers can betray anxiety as can blushing or perspiring. I once did an examination for discovery of a client's separated spouse. (Beforehand, he told me that she would blush when she lied.) Sure enough, at one point we were talking about some innocuous matter and I looked at her and a line of red began to move up her neck and into her face. The colour contrast was startling. From then on, I made note of every time that the rush of colour came on and compared that later with the instructions that my client had given me. I knew that this would be a significant part of my cross-examination at trial; however, the case settled before we made it that far.

When dealing with non-verbal indicators, it is usually best to simply acknowledge them.

I can see by the way that you are chewing on your collar that this topic makes you a little upset.

The client can then fill you in on why she is upset by the topic—or she may just explain it away by saying something silly. Whichever, it presents an opportunity to establish lines of trust between you and the client and to keep the dealings in the open, rather than have these things continually and subtly affect your interactions.

One caution to be observed is to think about what you say, using the active listening approach. Do not fall into the trap of parroting meaningless expressions like, "I know what you mean" or "I hear what you're saying." These trite statements are the legal world's equivalent to "Have a nice day." Avoid them. Don't tell a paraplegic that you know how he feels, because no one but a paraplegic could possibly know how he feels. If you want to know how being rendered a paraplegic has affected this person's life, then ask him, "How has the accident affected your life?" A straight, unpatronizing question will almost always get you a straight answer.

The cute expressions that sound good and come tripping off of the tongue will rarely serve the cause of accurate information gathering.

> **"Do not fall into the trap of parroting meaningless expressions like, 'I know what you mean' or 'I hear what you're saying.' These trite statements are the legal world's equivalent to 'Have a nice day.' Avoid them."**

"Platitudes beget platitudes. They had meaning at one time, but through overuse they have ceased to have any real meaning."

Platitudes beget platitudes. They had meaning at one time, but through overuse they have ceased to have any real meaning. The speaker is often unaware that they have actually made the comment.

You should try to reflect the emotional content of the client's information as well and as accurately as you outline the hard data. We are not talking about legal assistants "fixing" emotional problems—at least not any more than the problems can be fixed by legal solutions. It is also not your job to place a value judgment on the emotion—it needs to be acknowledged, but it is not an issue to be solved by the law office.

Active listening is essentially the opposite of an argument—the active listener avoids competition for conversational space. After all, though an argument is about communication, each speaker in an argument is often interested only in what he or she is trying to communicate. The current "listener" chomps at the bit, waiting to comment, not expending any energy listening to what is being said by the speaker.

Bob: *You're late again. Where were you?*

Sally: Ya, and it's good to see you, too.

Bob: *Well, I've been waiting here for 20 minutes in the rain. You knew I was on a tight schedule.*

Sally: Have you ever tried to get a cab on a rainy Friday afternoon?

Bob: *I don't know how I'm going to get all my work finished today. This really puts me behind the eight ball.*

Sally: My new sweater is ruined. I never brought a coat, and I could have just gone right to lunch next door to my office, but I waited for a stupid cab in the rain for half an hour.

Bob: *My boss just doesn't understand that quality work takes time. You can't just pump it out like gasoline.*

Sally: Do you want to order lunch or just forget the whole thing?

Bob: *Whatever.*

Sally: Ya, whatever.

All of this, of course, could have been avoided if only Bob and Sally had practised active listening.

With active listening there are two cardinal rules.

1.   You always have to *respond to the speaker's comment*, showing that you heard and understood the content.

2.   You have to *acknowledge the emotional content* of the comment. If you don't, it will keep returning, and the speaker will never be satisfied they have actually been heard.

How you view a situation depends on your perspective. The conversation between Bob and Sally might have gone like this:

Bob: *You're late again. Where were you?*

Sally: I know, I'm terribly sorry. And you look wet and hungry, you poor dear, let's step inside and we can trade stories about our terrible days while they get us some nice soup.

Bob: *Well, I've been waiting here for 20 minutes in the rain. I'm not sure we'll have time to eat, I'm on a tight schedule.*

Sally: I know, I know, I should have left even earlier, but I just didn't think I'd be standing in the rain for half an hour waiting for a cab.

Bob: *Oh gosh, I'm sorry I didn't even notice, you're soaked through. Let's get inside and warm you up.*

Sally: Are you sure you can manage? We can always reschedule.

Bob: *No problem. My boss is in a snit, but he'll never appreciate me anyway, so I'd rather spend time with you. The work will always be there when I get back.*

Sally: Good, let's console each other. Oh, by the way, my treat, I got a coupon.

Bob: *That's great.*

Now, you ask, isn't this simply a tawdry dramatization to make a cheesy point? True. But there is a learning point here: by actually responding to the content of the speaker's words, she or he feels heard and does not have the need to keep repeating the same chorus to try to get some reaction.

By responding to your client's emotional content, she feels validated and appreciated. Somebody cares how she feels. This makes the interviewer much more inclined to care about how the client feels. At that point, if you don't make your own caring response, you may feel as if you have behaved inappropriately—and most people want to avoid seeming inept or uncaring. So, it starts to be a two-way conversation, a two-way relationship.

How can you respond? Well, you can rephrase the client's comments, to let her know you get her point. If your client tells you she is sick and tired of nosey, officious pencil-pushers, you can empathize with her frustration in dealing with bureaucrats. If she tells you she doesn't think she has the energy to carry on with the litigation, you can tell her that you appreciate that the process is slow and cumbersome, but that together you'll get through it.

As a final point on the topic of active listening, you should encourage your client to be active in her role as well. So, give your client permission to interrupt, if a question or statement is not clear, and at the end of each sequence of information, ask your client if she has any questions or if she has anything to add.

> **"Active listening is essentially the opposite of an argument."**

In phrasing your invitation, use words that suggest you want to be sure you understand fully, rather than words that make your client feel it was her problem. People don't like feeling stupid.

I'm sorry, I'm not very knowledgeable about cars. When you said the fender just flew off while you were driving, can you explain a bit more about how that happened?

Always remember the basis for the interview: it is information gathering, to assist in providing legal services. The greater the understanding that you generate with the client, the more she will feel glad that she came to your firm in the first place, for help in solving her legal concern. Problem solving in as fast and cost-effective manner as possible is the ultimate goal.

Think of active listening as communicating three things:

- Interest

- Understanding

- Concern

"You can rephrase the client's comments, to let her know you get her point."

MIRRORING

Mirror questions are a relatively passive technique, since they add no content to the interview. The idea is simply to reflect back the content of what the speaker has said. You do so in hope that your client will confirm the intention of her statement, correct an impression that she now realizes she gave you, or expand on the topic. The mirror question is a valuable technique, but it has two main drawbacks.

1. Repetition, if overused, can be annoying. If you just repeat what the client has told you, with no modification, it is little more than a child's aggravating game of copying.

Adult:	*So, what are you up to?*
Child:	So, what are you up to?
Adult:	*Now, don't be goofy.*
Child:	Now, don't be goofy.
Adult:	*Now it's time to stop this.*
Child:	Now it's time to stop this.
Adult:	*I'm just an idiot.*
Child:	Yes, you are.

Someone parroting back what you say to them is infuriating. You can, however, do this in a valuable way—without driving your client crazy—by changing the wording.

Client: My boss talked to me in a very upsetting manner.

Interviewer: *Something your boss said upset you?*

Client: Yes, well, he accused me of lying.

Interviewer: *He said you weren't being truthful in something you said?*

Client: Yes, it was about my expense account.

Interviewer: *Your boss accused you of falsifying your expense account?*

Client: Exactly.

You see from this example that the conversation is kept focused by the questions. Not only do they reflect back the content, but they direct the client to provide important detail. So the question, "Something your boss said upset you?" is designed to find out what the boss actually said, to take the client further into the content. Mirror questions can be used in combination with open questions, while keeping the client on track and assuring her you appreciate what she is saying. These techniques are additive: they support and enhance each other, to improve the overall interview.

By summarizing a client's information, she hears what she has said, can reflect on how it has been understood by you, and correct or modify any misunderstandings before they become fixed in your mind or in the process of the law firm's representation. Summarizing can happen a number of times, but don't overdo the frequency.

2. Repetition, by itself, does not provide any real response to the client. Any speaker looks for feedback, confirmation, and support. In addition, if you use only mirror questions, you will be very limited in the information that you acquire.

EMPATHIC RESPONSES

A client is, by definition, a person who comes to you with needs. Part of these needs often include an emotional component, sometimes obvious, sometimes hidden. At times, you ask yourself: what is this person really getting at? what is the *hidden agenda*? At other times you may feel as if you are being beaten over the head by this person's needs. Regardless, one thing is certain: unless you deal with the emotional content, it will interfere with the "legal" content. If you ignore it or evade it, due to your own discomfort with "touchy-feely" matters, it is going to come back and bite you, often at the worst possible time.

As mentioned before, when the emotional content of the client's concerns are ignored, the client will keep bringing them up, keep trying to get the interviewer's attention for a response. Students have commented, after an interview, "He kept bringing up his anger—he couldn't get past

> **"By summarizing a client's information, she hears what she has said, can reflect on how it has been understood by you, and correct or modify any misunderstandings before they become fixed in your mind or in the process of the law firm's representation."**

it." This, of course, is more a comment on the interviewer's failure to deal with this emotional issue, possibly because he didn't think it was *legally* significant. If you hear a comment repeated, don't dismiss it. You can be sure the client hasn't.

A law office is not a therapist's office. Legal professionals are neither trained for nor paid to solve client's emotional concerns, but solving their legal concerns usually moves clients a great distance toward resolving their emotional turmoil. Yet, without some level of emotional interchange, most clients will feel alienated, untrusting, timid, and/or frustrated, even with good legal representation. In many instances, you are the front line in client services, and if the clients are comfortable and happy with your representation, they will be happy with the services they get from the firm.

The road to empathy starts well before you meet any particular client; it originates in how you relate to people in general and clients in particular. Like many other professionals, lawyers tend to objectify clients and categorize them in relation to their "problems." In law offices, clients can be described as "cases," in other words the client's legal entanglement defines her being. The client is no longer Sally with the sunny disposition and good sense of humour, but the "moderate whiplash case." John Mortimer's character, *Rumpole of the Bailey*, refers to his clients as "a slight spot of larceny over in the Oxbridge Magistrate's Court."

Even by referring to client concerns as "problems," we cast them in an unpleasant light. It is as if the clients bring us trouble when they come to us, rather than justifying our existence and paying us well for it. Any client should be welcomed and valued, not made to feel that she is spoiling our otherwise good day. Lawyers sometimes joke that the practice of law would be great if only we could eliminate the clients. Some teachers, doctors, and other professionals speak in these terms, perhaps funny to those on the inside, but not a message that should, in any way, be communicated to clients. So try to avoid the use of the term "problem" when asking clients about their legal concerns. It takes a conscious effort, but it helps to keep matters in the proper perspective.

Empathy is not easy. It has some of the feel of sympathy, but it is more communicating a sense that you can *understand* what the client is going through—placing yourself in the shoes of the other person. However, this rarely works, unless it is genuinely experienced; it comes across as phony. It's like the trainee at the fast-food joint, who is taught to say, "Have a nice day." It is meaningless, because it is not connected to any relationship with the listener or sense of genuine concern. But you can communicate empathy through your responses to the client.

Much is communicated through your body posture and attentiveness. Eye contact and facial expressions can be as open and supportive as words, in certain circumstances. Verbal acknowledgment of the client's difficult circumstances will go a long way to making a connection on an empathic level. Modulations of voice can cut through barriers; the softening of your voice implies intimacy and caring, even if you are talking about the terms of a settlement agreement.

Being aware of the speed of your communication helps establish a better rapport. One mistake that's often made is to rush through "stuff" you know by heart, like outlining the purpose of the interview or giving assurances of confidentiality. Some interviewers even mumble their names in the initial interview. Now, think about the client. She knows she was told your name, but doesn't remember it, because she never heard it clearly. You created the embarrassment.

It is important to pace yourself, making an effort to connect with the client. Why should a client bare her soul to someone who doesn't care about them as a person? Because it is in her best interest? That is not good enough. These are emotions, which are not particularly subject to rational control.

In every legal interview, there is what I call an empathic moment. It is often the moment in the interview when the client mentions the issue that brought her to your law office—and it may actually precede her specific legal concern. How you respond to that moment will determine, to a great extent, how your client feels about you. There may, in fact, be more than one empathic moment, and the first "revelation" may be a test, to see what your reaction is—or whether you react at all.

> I slipped on the ice and came down hard on my elbow.

> I heard voices in the room. When I entered, they were naked on my bed.

> I've worked in this industry for 10 years, and I've finally saved enough money to buy my own shop.

As you can see from the third example, empathic moments are not always unhappy events; however, given the nature of our work, they often are. The main point here: every empathic moment requires a response. I have often seen students do client interviews where the client reveals a very traumatic event—"The vehicle careened around the corner, striking me from behind while I was in the crosswalk"—and, without looking up from his writing pad, the student–interviewer asks, "What was the date of that accident?"

Think about your client. You don't seem to give a damn about her being thrown through the air, crashing down on the pavement, lying helpless in the cold November rain, blood streaming into the gutter. Don't kid yourself that your reaction does *not* affect the quality of your client's information. It does.

Responses to the client do not need to be gushy or "over the top." As an interviewer, you are not expected to weep or go to great lengths to lament the client's misfortune. However, some expression of understanding about her difficulties is called for. So, imagine a comment like, "When I lost my job, I seemed to lose my bearings." That should inspire a response like, "I know, it can be terribly disorienting when this happens." And the level of response should be tied to the relative size of the calamity.

> When I caught my heel in the grate and fell, I twisted my ankle and ruined my new stockings.

Your response might be, "That must have been upsetting." However, if a client tells you that her child contracted AIDS from a blood transfusion, your empathic

"Empathy is not easy. It has some of the feel of sympathy, but it is more communicating a sense that you can *understand* what the client is going through—placing yourself in the shoes of the other person."

response must be commensurate. "Oh, how horrible. Do you need a minute before we continue?" Generally, clients are not looking for sympathy but merely an indication that you understand the importance of the events—and that you give a damn. The empathic response helps eliminate obstacles to communication.

Just as the interviewer needs to understand the client, the client needs to understand the interviewer. This implies that you will be alert to the language proficiency of the client, her ethnic or cultural background, and other factors. When you first meet, you may know very little about the client; however, you may detect how comfortable a person is with language, and thus modify the way you present your questions.

Your client may have difficulty talking about a certain matter. Try saying, "I realize this is very difficult for you." Something this simple can have the effect of verbally loosening her up and get the words flowing. At the same time, telling a client who has just experienced the death of her child, "I know where you are coming from" is likely to get you punched in the mouth, some would say deservedly.

Acknowledging the difficulty, showing concern for the client by offering coffee, tissues, or water is often all that is required. For the period she is in your office, for the period you are dealing with her, she should feel appreciated, respected, and professionally cared for in all her contact with you. As a professional, you can and will learn to care about a client's concerns—and to communicate that caring. But don't take it on yourself; don't carry it around on your shoulders day and night.

> **"The empathic response helps eliminate obstacles to communication."**

In a professional caring relationship, you can, indeed must, place a limit on your caring role. It is a nine-to-five responsibility, which must not be allowed to sap your energy. You do have your own life and loved ones.

Empathy has a place in the law office but it is something to use consciously where and to the degree that it fits. The anecdote about the kidnapped child on page 79 does not represent a lesson on how to deal with clients in crisis, or the triumph of maternal love over emotion; it does represent an argument for timing and choosing the degree of empathy in consideration of the overall circumstances—the big picture. Neither empathy nor sympathy would have done the latter client any good, if her ex had crossed into Alberta.

> **"Just as the interviewer needs to understand the client, the client needs to understand the interviewer."**

Listening, really listening, to clients is not hard. It can be exhausting, but it should not be difficult. The legal entanglements that clients bring to law firms are truly interesting—and, of course, of vital importance to the client.

During a law school competition, a student was doing a role-playing interview with an actor–client who had been recently widowed. At one point, the student–interviewer asked this woman, "Exactly when did your husband croak?" I almost swallowed my teeth. After the interview, I asked the competitor about his interesting choice of words. He perked up right away. "Oh, yes, well I did that consciously, since she was looking so depressed. I thought I would try to lighten things up a little." In spite of being well intentioned, he obviously had a different read on empathy than I did.

When I first became a lawyer, I had a client whom I saw through various trials and tribulations with her ex-husband, a manipulative and petty man. Over the course of a year, my client called me up every weekend with a crisis. The situation did not seem as simple as telling her not to call me at home, because many of her crises were real; for example, when her separated husband was banging down her door. All I could do was tell her to call the police, but in her distress, she needed me to confirm what was appropriate. At other times, I would be telling her that, yes, she had to get her children to go for access visits; otherwise, her husband would turn that against her.

The difficulty I had was that her phone calls did have a legal dimension; she wasn't just looking for emotional support. As with most clients, *immediately* is not soon enough when it comes to their concerns. Finally, I came to the point where I did have to tell her to only call me in a dire emergency. I had to outline what had not been an emergency in the past three or four weeks. She was very needy, and I found that I began to dread my weekends, and to fear hearing the telephone ring, particularly if it was close to her children's access times. My weekends had ceased to be what they are supposed to be—a respite from work and returning to work—and on Mondays, I felt emotionally exhausted. I was approaching the point where I would be no good to any of my clients.

Another client's estranged spouse had just kidnapped their child and was likely headed from Vancouver to Alberta. He had been gone for about three hours when her call came. I had to be in court on another urgent matter, at 2 p.m.; it was 10:45 when her call came to me. After failing to enlist any other legal service, I agreed to take the client, provided she could get to my office within half an hour. She did. She was terribly distraught, and I tried to let her know that I appreciated how difficult this was for her. We sat down to do the affidavit in support of an *ex parte* order that the children be returned to her and that the various police forces assist to that end.

We needed to give some history, along with the circumstances of the children coming into the father's care, and why she believed that he had absconded with them, etc. We needed to have this information before the Supreme Court judge right away, and I needed to be in court elsewhere at 2 p.m. Thank goodness we were not dealing with today's filing requirements, but it was still a tremendous challenge to get the paperwork completed with such time pressure. We reached a point when my client started to weep uncontrollably. For her, the situation was terrifying; she felt like she was going to lose her children. I then did something incredibly insensitive, but not uncaring. I told her in a fairly stern voice that if she couldn't pull herself together, we would never get the order, and her ex-husband would "escape" with the children. On the other hand, if she could get herself together, we would likely get the order and have a very good chance of stopping him. She was remarkable. Right before my eyes, she visibly sucked back her emotion, bottled it up tightly, and proceeded to answer my questions (about very emotional topics) so we could get the affidavit done.

We completed the affidavit and, as I ran from my office toward the courthouse, a few blocks away, I shouted over my shoulder, "OK, you can let go now." I was ushered into the judge's chambers, where he interrupted his sandwich break to hear me run through the circumstances, scanned the order I had drafted, and signed it. The fleeing husband was stopped by the RCMP at the border, and the children were returned to their mother overnight.

If you are finding the issues brought to you by clients boring, or you feel put upon by clients when they bring their concerns to you, then you are not exploring the issues effectively. The various legal concerns encountered in a law firm can very quickly become old hat—just another will, or house transfer, or motor vehicle accident. Be warned: you have missed what is unique in your client's circumstance. There is a whole tapestry of actions and emotions that have led this client to seek legal advice, at this very moment. You should feel a challenge to personalize this legal issue, so that you truly understand the significance of this to your client at this time. Then you can serve her well.

CHAPTER QUESTIONS

1. How can you demonstrate active listening to a client?

2. How would you deal with a client's use of inappropriate language in an interview?

3. What is empathy? Give an example of an empathic response.

4. What problems are associated with recording interviews with clients?

5. Discuss your perception of the reliability of a person's non-verbal communication.

CHAPTER EXERCISES

1. In pairs, students should go to a location where some sort of activity is taking place—in a gym, cafeteria, or parking lot. Without discussing the scene, each student writes for 10 minutes about what they observe. Compare the two descriptions. Look at the difference in content. Is there a different perspective operating? Did one or another miss some significant detail? Did one or another focus on a particular aspect? Later, the students could share their observations with the class, and the class may have additional observations or comments regarding the two versions of the common experience.

2. *Non-verbal communication exercise.* During the next week, make note of two situations where body language was instrumental in communicating. Note whether the non-verbal communication was intended or unintended.

3. *Listening exercises.* This exercise involves two students. One is given a topic to speak about; the other is given the chore of subtly interrupting the speaker's train of thought. The speaker's topic should be an opinion piece, like why they favour or oppose the death penalty. The listener should sit opposite the speaker and periodically gaze distractedly around the room, cross her arms,

lean forward or backward, smile or frown when the speaker makes a point, yawn, interrupt with an irrelevant question ("Did you see that movie where Bruce Willis plays the dead guy?") and in any other way that comes to mind. Afterward, the speaker should complete a questionnaire or respond to questions from a third party such as,

a. How do you feel you did in getting your point across?

b. Did the listener agree or disagree with your opinion?

c. Were there any communication inhibitors present?

d. Is there anything you would do differently?

4. Find a partner. Have your partner tell you a story about her life, what she did on her summer holiday, her most memorable experience. The listener should restate what the speaker has told her, such as, "So, the favourite part of your holiday was … ?" or, "I gather that the experience was … ." After you finish, ask the speaker:

a. Were your summaries accurate?

b. Did it help the telling of the story to have the feedback?

c. Could you have phrased your comments differently, for greater impact?

CHAPTER 6

Questioning Techniques

In Brief

This chapter examines questioning style as well as setting out specific types of questions. We also consider how to utilize questioning strategies, to maximize the effectiveness of the interview.

There are many ways by which you can elicit information from a client. The method you use should not be random but the result of a conscious choice of what approach is best at any particular stage in the interview. Of course, the questioning strategy will change as you proceed, even from one question to the next, but the approach should always be based on an intelligent choice, rather than whatever happens to pop into your head.

The interviewing process is a team effort, and the client should feel part of that process—an active participant in resolving his legal concerns. Open questions are the best way I have found to get the client actively involved from the very start of the process.

The main problem with most legal interviews is that too many narrow or leading questions are asked. I am a big fan of open questions. Naturally, not all questions can be open; that would lead to paralysis. But the proportion of open questions should be much greater than it typically is. However, let's begin exploring open questions.

OPEN QUESTIONS

In open or open-ended questions, the client is free to provide whatever information he feels is appropriate in response to a question. A question like, "How are you today?" is an open question.

Some people think that an open question cannot direct the client to a subject area. This is not so. If you ask, "What has brought you here today?" that is a perfectly good, open question to start the interview with—your client can choose what content to provide. Particularly in the early stages of an interview, this is important: open questions give the client the maximum opportunity to tell the law firm what he feels is important.

Open questions have disadvantages. If a client is excessively talkative, you may need to narrow the questions. (Troublesome clients are discussed in some detail in chapter 8.) Also, where a client lacks memory, open questions may net little information. Caution: there is a difference between lacking memory and shyness or reluctance to talk. With shy people, open questions are often, even precisely, what are called for to draw them out.

Limiting the use of open questions also applies to the client who has no grasp of what is relevant to his legal proceeding. With this type of client, it is usually a simple matter to direct him to the important issues. Look at the following examples of questioning sequences, to see if this point is clear.

Could you tell me what has brought you here today?

I want a divorce.

OK. Would you tell me what leads you to this conclusion?

I just don't trust my wife any more.

Tell me more about that.

Well, I think she's been sleeping around on me.

What makes you think this?

She spends a lot of time at her book club.

Is there anything else that leads you to this conclusion?

Ya, some of the books they read are pretty racy.

Have you spoken to your wife about your suspicions?

Not really, but why would a woman her age be reading dirty books?

Would you be interested in finding this out from her?

Do you think she would tell me, if I asked?

I don't know your wife. What do you think?

I guess it would be worth a try.

Now let's look at this from another approach.

So I understand that you want a divorce.

That's right. I do.

When were you married?

January 12, 1994.

What is your wife's maiden name?

Harlequin.

Her birth date?

July 4, 1969.

Have you separated?

Yes, on June 15.

Do you know where we can serve her?

At her mother's place, I suspect.

You're not likely to reconcile are you?

No way. I don't trust her.

OK. Come in tomorrow and we'll have the papers drawn up.

Great, that's very efficient.

We try to be.

These examples are presented to show that open questions require the client to think and provide detail. He is a part of the process, involved in providing information that will help your law firm assess the best way to serve his interests. Even in the first example, the client is not immediately forthcoming. Often, clients must be encouraged, even made to work at providing important information. But be aware that some come with the attitude that it is your job to get the right information out of them.

Occasionally, you will suspect a client of taking perverse pleasure in making you chase around with the wrong information, because you have neglected to ask the right questions. (They are smugly fiddling while Rome burns.)

"Your client is a valuable ally."

Another client may come to an interview all fired up to talk about his concerns. Such a client starts to tell his story, one that he has mentally rehearsed multiple times. Within a few heartbeats, the interviewer—often a student—interrupts the client with a question designed to extract some detail: "What was the date? Do you know where she lives? What is his full name?" The result? The interviewer has broken the client's train of thought and sent a message to the client that "I know what is important here and it's up to me to get the facts that I need." The client usually resumes his story, only to be interrupted again. "What colour was the car? Did you get a licence plate number?" The client often gives an involuntary look of annoyance and provides the information requested.

As the process of interrupting goes on, the client then visibly withdraws from the interview, pulling back in his seat, crossing his arms, giving increasingly short answers, and generally adopting a resigned or defeated posture, sometimes even becoming hostile to the interviewer.

Your client is a valuable ally. Listen to him. By not cutting him off, you help reaffirm the importance of what he has to say. By following up on what he says, you make the client part of the process, a partner in solving his legal issues.

CLOSED/NARROW QUESTIONS

Closed questions are useful when you want to elicit specific information. A closed or narrow question leaves little room for interpretation by the client. It is very specific and requires a specific, usually short, answer. What colour was the car? How tall was the assailant? How long have you worked there? All of these questions can and will be important—at the right stage. However, if you ask what colour the car was before learning whether the vehicle was a car or a truck or a minivan, chances are you'll be searching for a light blue, late-model Ford car, instead of a light blue, late-model Ford pickup truck.

If you summarize or reward a client's information and invite him to correct any mistakes, he will likely do so. But if you use a series of direct, one-word, response-type questions, the mistake may never come to light.

To summarize: narrow questions have an important role at the appropriate stage of an interview, but be selective in using them. Novice interviewers often assume that a client's pause is an indication that the "open-ended approach" is not working. Waiting for the client to find the right word or thought is wonderful way to show him that you expect thoughtful participation, that the quality of his answer is important. So, be patient.

The most limited form of the narrow-question style is the yes/no question. We have often heard a cross-examiner say, "Just answer the question, yes or no." Sometimes this is out of frustration with a witness who is determined to advance his point of view at every opportunity. That said, few significant questions can be answered with a yes/no response. Restricting a witness in this way is likely to misinform the judge, by excluding valuable information.

Like either/or questions (later in this chapter), yes/no questions miss out on a huge area of responses that are "sorta yes" and "sorta no." For most of us, the world is not black or white.

In some circumstances, narrow questions, even yes/no questions, at an early stage in an interview, may be of use. If the client is so nervous he is frozen, then a few basic questions can help. If you ask such a client where he lives or how to spell his name, he thinks, "Hey, I can answer to that one." You can start with questions that only require one-word answers, and slowly move to more lengthy and challenging questions, as the client appears to loosen up. The sooner you

> ## "A closed or narrow question leaves little room for interpretation by the client."

In a client-counselling competition at law school, my partner and I had different responsibilities: she would greet the client, make him comfortable, and orient him to the interview process, and I would then launch into the substance of his legal concern. In one particular interview, when she finished her introduction, I asked the client to tell us what brought him to see us that day. The client was about a minute and a half into his description of events when my partner interrupted, saying, "Sorry to interrupt here, but I forgot to ask, did you have any trouble finding parking today?" (This was one of the icebreakers we were using in the introductory phase.) I probably looked at her as if she were insane, but the client mumbled some polite response, and we carried on with the interview. My partner was obviously just nervous and, in the end, this was only a minor mistake; however, it is vital to be in the moment with the client and listen to what he has to say. There is no agenda that is more important than what concerns the client.

progress to open questions, the better. Appendix F lists some examples of open-ended and closed question starters.

PROBING QUESTIONS

Probing questions may be open or closed. They often follow from a client's answer and can be characterized as "why" questions.

> *Why did you hire Frank as your contractor?*
>
> *Why do you want to cut your son out of your will?*
>
> *Why did you leave your wife?*

With these questions, you pursue your understanding of the circumstances surrounding an event—and, obviously, the client's motivation. The danger is that "why" questions tend to have a value component.

By asking "why?" you may give the impression that you disapprove, that you think the client is in the wrong. "Why did you leave your wife?" might be heard as, "Why did you go and leave a perfectly good woman?"—not really what that client wants to hear. "Why did you hire Frank as a contractor?" can be interpreted as, "What kind of idiot would hire that incompetent person? I guess you got what you deserved." Try to ensure that your probing questions do not have any judgmental or value component. This may depend on the tone of voice you use or the context at that stage of the interview.

> *Can you tell me about the events that led to the house fire?*
>
> *Describe what led to your relationship coming to an end.*

Keep in mind that the circumstances that led to the events (which brought the client to your office) are what you want to discover, not who is at fault or if it could have been handled better. To the extent that blaming will happen, there is another time and place for that.

Probes do not have to be in a "why" format; they can be as simple as guttural responses, *uh-huh* or *carry on, yes, tell me more.* These are all probes and can be quite effective in drawing the client out on certain matters. Imagine your psychoanalyst saying "Yes, I see." Even silence can be a probe, although you need to monitor its effect carefully.

If silence is not being effective in prompting the client to fill in the gaps, continuing use of it will kill any flow in the interview—and perhaps leave the client wondering whether you know what you are doing.

Probing questions can take the form of a hypothetical question. In this style of inquiry, you describe a hypothetical situation to the client, then you ask a question like, "How would you respond to that?" or "What would you do in this circumstance?"

> *Let's say that Widget Co. agreed to supply the sprockets at the same price as you thought they were committed to, provided you gave them a purchase order for your full year's requirements. Would that be satisfactory to you?*

"Few significant questions can be answered with a yes/no response."

You can see that this form of question is valuable in dealing with negotiated or mediated resolutions to conflicts. Hypothetical questions assist in determining the parameters of the client's response to certain situations, enabling the law firm to chart a course of action that may result in an early resolution to the conflict.

Some probing questions are confrontational. These are most often seen in hierarchical interviews, such as disciplinary meetings or interrogations. A cross-examination in a courtroom is typically confrontational, at least in part. The use of confrontation in client interviewing is very questionable. On the one hand, a client may not be cooperating in the manner you would hope, may even be obviously misleading you. But to (essentially) accuse him of lying is likely to generate a hostile or defensive reaction, making it harder to obtain the information required to assist him. If the rare situation occurs where you think it necessary to confront a client, this is a decision for the lawyer to make, not one you should pursue on your own.

Responsive probes are slightly different from hypothetical questions. In a responsive-probe scenario, you put a proposition to your client.

Police officers often use the technique of asking chatty, innocuous questions of a suspect who is disinclined to talk to them about the crime they are investigating. The officer starts by asking the suspect's name. You pretty well have to answer that one. Then for the address. Well, why not? Then it's, "Is that near the bus station?" This has absolutely nothing to do with the crime. After three or four more questions that have nothing to do with the offence, the investigator will try one closer to home. If the suspect answers that one, even with an innocent explanation, then the officer asks another. The suspect feels it would be suspicious if he didn't answer that question, so he makes up a story, and soon he is trapped in a poorly constructed web of lies. Police investigators are usually experts in questioning, often with witnesses who don't want to be helpful. Since rubber truncheons are no longer in vogue, seducing the information out of an uncooperative suspect is one of the few tools left in their arsenal.

Some people choose to delay a bequest to children until they have reached a certain age. How do you feel about this?

Settlement agreements often include a penalty for disclosure of the terms of the agreement. Is this something that you are interested in?

In both of the above examples, the interviewer provides some information to the client and, in obtaining a reaction to the probe, is better able to determine the next steps to take.

Probing questions are designed to get at aspects of the incident that have not come out in the witness's version of events. This type of question should cause the client to stretch himself, to think about aspects he may never have thought about—and they often result in valuable additional information.

You can provide a valuable contribution to the fact-gathering process by using your own knowledge base to help you connect with the client and get at the facts. For example, in a recent student interview, the role-playing client was a dog breeder who had a dispute with a kennel. Having seen the film *Best In Show* could be the basis for some small talk and a starting point for understanding the situation and the client's concerns.

I saw the film Best In Show. *Now, I'm not sure whether it depicted dog breeding realistically, but it struck me as an intense vocation. What are the financial costs and rewards of dog breeding?*

As you can see, the key to closed or narrow questioning is a healthy curiosity, following up on the threads from the client's initial outline of facts. Doing this with a plan or focus—while avoiding the temptation to jump right in to directive and leading questions—is an art. This technique is valuable, an art form that is particularly worth cultivating in legal interviewing.

LEADING QUESTIONS

These are the extreme form of narrow questions. With a leading question, the interviewer proposes a fact to her client, and the client either agrees or disagrees with it. The answer is contained in the question, and the client does not need to provide any substance with his answer.

Imagine the following cross-examination during a trial.

You went to the beach to watch the fireworks display?

Yes.

And you had not had anything to drink when you headed down there?

No.

When you were at the beach, some loud, drunken teenagers caught your attention?

Yes.

And you went over to them and politely asked them to keep their voices down?

Yes.

And without any form of provocation, they viciously attacked you, giving you a broken jaw and puncturing your lung.

That's right.

And you see two of your attackers at counsel table, looking very smug and defiant.

You bet.

Now, aside from the fact that the other lawyer must have been deaf or asleep during this entire examination not to object, the problem with this questioning is that none of the substantive evidence comes from the witness. All of the content is supplied by the lawyer, so how can the judge or jury give it any weight?

A legal interview is not in-court testimony, but it is just as important in a law-office interview that the information come out of the client's mouth, not the interviewer's. Perhaps it's even more important: if you interview the client before the lawyer gets to speak with him, a misstatement of the facts may become ingrained by the time the lawyer hears it. It can be easy to lead a client astray with your questioning, particularly where he has, consciously or subconsciously, accepted the "correct" answers that you have provided in your leading questions.

And you didn't have more than two beers before getting into your car.

Aaaa … ya, that's right, less than two.

Then you pulled over as soon as the police signalled, just before midnight, am I right?

Ya, right, that's the ticket.

The influence of leading questions can be intended or unintended, and the impact on the client can be conscious or subconscious.

> **"The influence of leading questions can be intended or unintended, and the impact on the client can be conscious or subconscious."**

Another problem is where the leading question is not quite right but almost right. Whether the client corrects your version depends on a number of factors, including the client's personality, how the question is phrased, how tired the client is, or whether the client just wants to get through the interview before he gets a parking ticket.

Take the situation where your client had his foot run over at about 4:30 p.m. on Tuesday of last week by a 1991 grey van, whose wheel cut across the sidewalk at the corner. Your client was waiting for the light to change, so he could enter the crosswalk. He did not see the driver of the van because there were no windows on the side of the van, and he crumpled up in pain after the wheel ran over his foot. There was, however, a woman who immediately came to his aid. The interview is on a Thursday. Let's look at how leading questions might contaminate the communication.

1. *So, you were struck by a late-model, dark car last Tuesday?*

   Ahh … ya, that's right.

2. *This happened late in the day?*

   That's right.

3. *It was at a crosswalk?*

   That's right.

4. *And you had the light in your favour?*

   Sure.

5. *There were no passengers in the vehicle at the time?*

   I guess not.

6. *And the police said there were no witnesses?*

   That's right.

Question 1: The client doesn't see any need to correct the interviewer about the type of vehicle—car or van, what's the difference? Whether it's a late model or not is ambiguous: is 1991 a late model or an old vehicle? The client is not going to get into semantics. A similar problem exists with regard to the colour of the vehicle. Is grey dark or light? It may be halfway in between, or it may be dark grey or light grey, but your client, looking at you with your information file, is not about to challenge this assertion. Did the accident happen last Tuesday or this Tuesday? The interviewer might be more attuned to this possible error if she were listening rather than talking this much.

Question 2: What is late in the day? Is it day, evening, or night? How late is late?

Question 3: The client has been truthful that the accident was at a crosswalk, not *in* the crosswalk as the interviewer might—and perhaps does—assume.

Question 4: The answer to this question is either true or false, but by phrasing the question in this way, the interviewer encourages the client to answer "Sure," which is false. The van driver is at fault in this situation, so it does not matter whether the light was in the client's favour or not. However, by asking this question, the interviewer leads the client to make a false statement, which may be contradicted by the client's statement to the insurance company or by another witness. More important, the client's legitimate claim has been undermined by the introduction of an issue about his credibility—if he lies about a straightforward fact, can the rest of his testimony be trusted?

Question 5: The client has, this time, actually shown uncertainty, but the interviewer has not picked up on it. If she did, the whole confusion might begin to unravel—and the true circumstances come to light. Certainly the question "Did you see the driver of the vehicle?" would likely net better results.

Question 6: Again the client has answered truthfully, but the information is misleading. Yes, the police said there were no witnesses, but what about the woman who rushed to his aid? Did she see the accident? Does she happen to work in corner grocery store? Would she respond to one of those utility-pole notices seeking witnesses to accidents?

With leading questions, agreeable people tend to agree, and confrontational people tend to disagree. Clients are usually agreeable, which means they will be inclined to concur with any statements you put to them. They see members of the law firm as the experts, and who are they to disagree?

One of the few situations where leading questions can be useful is with clients who are being evasive. Sometimes, they need to be pinned down on details. This needs to be done in a non-threatening manner, but it can be accomplished effectively with leading questions.

How much alcohol did you consume that night?

"Leading questions are dangerous beasts and must be kept on a leash at all times. They have a use but are almost always more likely to be misused than used wisely."

Henry Ford revolutionized the world by mass producing the automobile. He made black Model T Fords. He did not, however, respond well to customer demand, and when he was pressed to make them in different colours, his response was, "Customers can have Model T's in any colour they wish, as long as it is black." In the end, customer demand won out, but the suggestion that customer wishes can be dictated by the manufacturer—buy it or don't buy it—is akin to limiting the client to two options in your search for the truth in any particular situation.

If we offer only two options, it's usually because we only see two possibilities. Our perspectives limit us. The client might have a third option, perhaps a fourth, but not either of the two we offer. Whenever only two options are offered, the possibility exists that the correct description or at least the more precise one is overlooked. Again, you risk misleading your client.

This question is perhaps only quasi-leading; it doesn't contain the answer—that is, the amount of alcohol the client consumed. However, it is leading in the sense that it contains the conclusion that the person had been drinking. This assumption, if it hasn't already been offered up, is leading. As I comment in chapter 8's section on troublesome clients, this type of questioning must be non-judgmental to be effective.

Leading questions are dangerous beasts and must be kept on a leash at all times. They have a use but are almost always more likely to be misused than used wisely.

EITHER/OR QUESTIONS

Either/or questions—where the client is offered a choice of two options—are also problematic. From the crosswalk scenario: "Was the car dark or light?" Well, of course, it can be neither dark nor light, but, as the Procol Harum song says, "a whiter shade of pale."

What's wrong with simply asking, "What colour was the vehicle?" The same applies to a question like, "Was he tall or short?" To a person who barely breaks five feet on tiptoes, most people look tall; but, to a basketball player, we are all shorties, even those of us who bang our heads on a six-foot doorway.

SEQUENCE IN QUESTIONING

The main principle here is that open and narrow questions, even leading and either/or questions, can be asked in sequence, for maximum effect. In the initial stages of an interview, a series of open questions are often the most-effective tactic. At some stage, however, you will find it necessary to shift into more specific questioning. One way to visualize this is called a funnel sequence, with the broad, open questions at first, narrowing into the more specific questions and possibly ending with yes/no or leading questions. Figure 6.1 shows a funnel sequence.

Question 1 is the most open. This is followed by a series of questions that narrow the focus, but they are still open; they all leave the client with considerable room to determine what important details to provide.

By the time the interviewer gets to question 6, she is being more direct in indicating which aspects the client should comment on.

Figure 6.1 A Funnel Sequence

1. *Tell me what has brought you here today?*
   My neighbour assaulted me.

2. *Can you tell me what led to this assault?*
   Well, it all has to do with his dog.

3. *Can you tell me more about that?*
   He got this new dog who is not trained at all, and it runs through my flower beds, digging up my roses.

4. *And then what happened?*
   I put barbed wire in with the roses to keep his dog out, and I caught my neighbour tearing up the wire the other day, so I turned my hose on and soaked him.

5. *What happened then?*
   He went nuts and came after me with a lawn jockey.

6. *Did you sustain any injuries?*
   You bet, I got a dislocated shoulder.

7. *Anything else?*
   Just a broken finger.

8. *When did this happen?*
   Last Friday.

9. *Can you tell me your neighbour's name?*
   Simon Legree.

Question 7 is designed to elicit important details from the client on significant aspects of the case.

Question 8 is very specific: she is looking for an exact date.

Question 9 seeks to identify the assailant—the defendant, if the case is to proceed to litigation.

The broad, open questions at the beginning allow the client to provide substantial detail that he deems important.

You can see that the client is made to do a little work during the process—and he owns up to some involvement in the incident, although he is never treated judgmentally. The funnel sequence of interviewing can and should be used repeatedly throughout the interview, to maximize the information provided by the client.

Questioning is a process of mining for information. Think of an exploratory gold mine. When the exploration company locates a vein, they mine that vein until it runs out. At that point, the search continues from where it left off, until another vein is struck and pursued. Thus, in an interview, all the important information on subtopics can be drawn out, at the same time keeping the exploration on track, ready to strike the motherlode.

To view the interview process in another way, think of primary and secondary questions. Primary questions open up a new area of discussion: "Tell me about your injuries"; secondary questions follow up on the initial question.

> *Describe the injuries to your neck.*

or

> *What has the doctor told you about your back?*

Start with a general question about a particular area, and follow that through in a thorough manner. This will net you plentiful and valuable information to use in representing your client.

Now, look at the following questioning sequence.

> 1. *What brought you here today?*

My neighbour assaulted me.

> 2. *What's your neighbour's name?*

Simon Legree.

> 3. *Can you tell me when this assault happened?*

Last Friday.

> 4. *Were you injured?*

Yes, my shoulder was dislocated.

> 5. *You didn't start the fight, did you?*

No way.

> 6. *And you want to sue him?*

You bet.

In this approach, the interviewer has immediately launched into very specific questions. Important information is overlooked in focusing on these specifics so early on, and the client has almost become a spectator, rather passively responding to such pointed questions. The final, leading questions are almost designed to inspire a denial of any involvement; they could even set the lawyer up for some rude surprises. The interviewer will obtain all the necessary information to complete a statement of claim to proceed with litigation, but she is missing the valuable information needed for effective representation of the client through the litigation process, including information that could result in legal advice to the client to abandon the thought of litigation.

SHOTGUN OR MULTIPLE QUESTIONS

A common interviewing error is to ask a series of detailed questions as a run-on sentence.

> *Now Mr. Woods, when you entered the room, what did you see—was it dark; did you notice the blood stain on the floor; who entered first?*

Believe it or not, interviewers seem to love these kinds of questions. The interviewer's mind races ahead and thinks of three or four things to ask and, instead of crafting a question, she simply plunks them all in random order into one sentence. This is very lazy and undisciplined. The problem with multiple questions is that they are confusing to the client. The answers can also be confusing to the interviewer—it is often unclear which of the responses relates to which question. This approach is just plain irritating to intelligent life. Govern yourself accordingly.

Rather than sliding into such undisciplined habits, choose one subject area and ask a question like, "Describe what you saw when you entered the room." Follow up, as necessary, depending on what the client tells you.

> *Can you tell me what the lighting was like in the room?*

And continue,

> *Describe the mark you noticed on the floor.*

And again,

> *Which of you entered the room first? (The client has said that they both entered the room.)*

By structuring the questions in this disciplined manner, the answers will be much clearer and more helpful.

VALUE-ADDED QUESTIONS

One final element regarding questioning needs attention. The language you use has great potential to influence the client, and your tone of voice and manner of presentation can affect how he responds. Parents often try this with children, usually with limited success.

> *Would you like to have that cold, sticky, runny ice cream or …
> br-r-r-occolli!!! Yeah, broccoli, yummy, yummy in our tummy.*

Aside from your child thinking you are an idiot, he only has to be burned once to wise up to the voice-inflection con. But the words alone, subtle or not, can draw the client in a particular direction. If you refer to your client's ex as the plaintiff or defendant, this distances him or her (from your client), depersonalizing that ex, and increasing the likelihood of frosty communications. Prosecutors invariably refer to the person who lodged the complaint against the accused as the "victim." The lawyer does this to psychologically entice the jury to align itself with the complainant—and if the jury buys into the description of the complainant as a victim, the prosecutor is halfway to making his case. A lawyer's choice of words is seldom accidental but can, of course, be persuasive.

> How fast was the car going when it careened past you?
>
> Where were you when you heard Mr. Grey screaming at his wife?
>
> Did you actually see the accused groping the child?

A car that *careens past* is, in most jurors' minds, going faster than a car that's *leaving the scene*. Someone seen *groping* a child is despicable, certainly nastier than someone hugging a child. The use of neutral language by an interviewer will help ensure that her biases and assumptions are not interjected into the description of what took place. The content of the interview is, therefore, much more reliable and helpful than if it is sculpted by the interviewer's language.

Lawyers also use language skillfully in order to introduce "facts" into evidence that have not been proven in court. In an assault trial, the Crown will ask what time the "assault" occurred, when, in many instances, the question whether the physical contact was voluntary has not been dealt with. It may stay an open question until the jury makes its ruling. Many prosecutors instinctively realize that the more they repeat the characterization of the appellant as a person who was assaulted, the more likely the jury is to see it that way. Because of its powerful influence on the fact-finding process, I refer to this technique as "sculpting" with questions.

"The use of neutral language by an interviewer will help ensure that her biases and assumptions are not interjected into the description of what took place."

I was prosecuting an impaired-driving charge once, and I was cross-examining the accused. His defence depended on a pattern of drinking that would mean that his Breathalyzer reading was wrong. An expert witness, listening to the evidence, was noting down the accused's pattern of drinking. I was testing his story. (He had stated that he had had two drinks, then went over to his friend's house. He was stopped by the police *after* leaving his friend's place, and, as long as he didn't drink there, the expert would testify that he would not be above the legal limit at the time of driving.) Everything was going smoothly for the accused, until I asked the question, "Did you have anything to drink subsequent to your arrival at your friend's home?" "Yes, I did," he answered— thereby tossing his defence to the wind. His lawyer looked shocked and half rose to his feet, stopping when he couldn't think of anything to object to. I had to laugh at this, but being Crown counsel, it would not be appropriate to take unfair advantage of the witness. English was not the accused's first language, and I suspected he had misunderstood the question. My next question was, "Did you have anything to drink after arriving at your friend's house?" His eyes got big, and he put his hand on his heart and swore on some dead relative that he did not. Regardless of the dramatic show, the point is that the witness did not understand the word *subsequent*, but, even so, that did not stop him from answering my question as if he did.

Be sure your language is clear; for example, don't use ambiguous terms or double negatives. When you get an answer from your client, you must be certain that your question was uncomplicated. If you ask,

> *As the proprietor of the business, were you not fully aware of the liabilities that you had for employee deductions?*

you should be scratching your head, if your client just answers yes or no. Let's look at a few other questions.

> *Were you not trying to avoid the collision?*
>
> *When you were dismissed, was it not unclear what the exact reasons were?*
>
> *Don't you want to answer my question?*
>
> *Would it not be true that you did not visit the deceased on the evening in question?*

You must phrase questions clearly, so that the answers you get are also clear.

MEMORY AIDS

Wilder Penfield, a Canadian neurosurgeon who pioneered research into surgical treatment of epilepsy, did experiments where he used mild electrical stimulation of the temporal lobes of a subject's brain. He discovered that probing specific locations on the temporal lobe caused a subject to experience vivid memories—visual, auditory, olfactory memories of events, in technicolour, surround-sound, smell-o-vision. These could be the most ordinary events, such as the view the subject had as a child from his bedroom window on a particular spring morning. What this says is that the brain is a vast repository of information that *can* be tapped with the right stimulation. Part of your job will entail stimulating the memory of clients about events that may be years in their past.

There are many methods that can assist in recovering memories. One way is to ask your client to visualize "the scene" and provide as much detail as possible. In constructing the scene, pointed questions will usually help.

> *When you visualize the scene, how many people do you see?*
>
> *Do you recall whether he was wearing anything on his head?*
>
> *Did you notice anything in his hand?*

You might ask your client to review a statement or notes, from the time of the incident, to see whether this refreshes his memory. Sometimes, you will have photographs or other materials on file that can help revive these memories. You must be careful to ensure that the information you obtain is an actual memory and not simply a repetition of someone else's statement or an interpretation of a photograph. The success of your client's legal action may hinge on your efforts.

Your questioning may assist a client in remembering what took place, but you must be careful that the client is not simply responding to suggestions you put forth. So, if your client is asked to describe a person and he states that she was "average," you may be able to assist with specific questions like, "How tall would you say she was?" If he again responds that she was "average," you might ask how she compared to his size or even your own size. You can ask about hair colour, tone of complexion, colour and style of clothing, any number of specific questions that will direct your client's attention to aspects of the other person that would help identify her.

A related issue, made public in the past decade by several news-making investigations and trials, is false memory syndrome. Even a brief synopsis would need several pages of text; however, the literature on that topic is extensive, and you should familiarize yourself with it. The key for you as an interviewer is to avoid any involvement with the client/witness that suggests, directs, or "plants" information during the interview process.

CROSS-EXAMINATION

Naturally, your client shouldn't feel as if he is being cross-examined by the law firm he has hired. Given that you are there to help your client, why do clients so often answer questions in ambiguous or evasive ways? Who knows? But you will often have to ask follow-up questions, when your client appears to have avoided answering the first question. In these circumstances, try to determine what caused the avoidance. Perhaps your client simply misunderstood the question. Think about your question—was it clear? Perhaps he is particularly sensitive to the topic. Is it embarrassing, or does it show him in a negative light? In these circumstances, the nonjudgmental assurance that the client should feel from you is key to getting to the bottom of the mystery. Perhaps it is too early in your relationship for the client to have the level of trust necessary to open up to you. One of your best approaches is to deal with the issue head on.

> *When I asked you if you had been drinking that night, you told me that*
> *your doctor has put you on strict orders not to drink. It is very impor-*
> *tant for us to know whether you had been drinking; otherwise, we can*
> *be blindsided at some point, and that will hurt your case. I should also*
> *remind you that everything you tell me is confidential. So, thinking*
> *carefully about this, had you consumed any alcohol that evening?*

You haven't called the client a liar. You are only gently testing him. But you have let him know how important the information is—and that the answer is confidential. And you will not be judgmental about his response, will you?

You must deal with contradictory information without a confrontation, which may cause the client to dig in.

> *I wonder if you could help me out with understanding this. You told me*
> *that you never touched the complainant, but the police report states*
> *that there is an impression of your signet ring on his right cheek. Is*
> *there something I am missing? or does that help you recall what*
> *happened that night?*

The object is not to trap the client in a lie but to point out the obvious—how another person, such as a judge, will respond to the information. By acting as a sounding board, you can provide him with a valuable service.

FOLLOWING UP ON THE INITIAL INTERVIEW

What happens after the initial interview varies depending on the approach taken in different law offices. Some have a questionnaire designed for the type of interview you have conducted, which you will complete and pass on to the lawyer responsible for the matter. Others require a memo to the responsible lawyer. If there isn't a questionnaire, you may want to create one. But whether you use a memo or questionnaire, having the information outlined in a standard format will aid the lawyer and other staff in locating information efficiently for future purposes. This information may be used in drafting pleadings or affidavits, or for preparing for other processes such as discoveries or even trial. The initial information that comes from the client is extremely important. It will affect how you represent the client and even the outcomes you can achieve for him.

A memo should provide complete identifying details regarding the client, a history of the client's concern, an outline of the legal issue, an indication of what stage in the process the dispute is at, and (if the lawyer you are working with is open to it) any suggestions you might have for what steps to take from here on. For example, it might not be immediately obvious that a particular witness is crucial and ought to be interviewed immediately—or even that a limitation is about to expire. *Never take a chance that the lawyer will catch a limitation without your mentioning it; it is just too serious to risk the exposure and disservice to the client.*

Once you have completed your initial interview, you may discover that there is more information you require. You will first need to decide whether you should do a follow-up interview right away, so you have the information before you pass the file back to the lawyer, or whether it would be better to have the lawyer review the file first, to see if there is even more information that you need to obtain. The more experienced you become, the more complete your initial interviews should be—and the less often this issue will arise. The advantage of getting the missing information before it goes to the lawyer is that she will then be able to have as complete a picture as possible when she initially reviews the file. The disadvantage is that if further information is required after you speak with the lawyer, you are *once more* telephoning the client, and the firm may look as if it didn't quite have its strategy organized in the first instance.

One way of taking the sting out of this is to tell the client in the initial interview that you will be contacting him from time to time, to supplement information obtained at the first meeting. This does not, however, get you too far if, for instance, you are calling back on a divorce case, asking if the client has a copy of the marriage certificate; or on an estate file asking for the name of the deceased; or other such oversights. In a case like those, you will simply have to use your charm. The follow-up contact may work more smoothly, if you gather your thoughts and ask all of your overlooked questions in one go.

Another valuable tool is the reporting letter to the client. This is particularly useful, if the client has committed to obtaining some necessary information or documentation to assist in the legal action. No matter how clear you were in the inter-

> **"The initial information that comes from the client is extremely important. It will affect how you represent the client and even the outcomes you can achieve for him."**

view, the client may very well "blank out" on his commitment to provide more information the moment he leaves your office. However, the corporate memory must be flawless; otherwise, valuable information is lost. A reporting letter that summarizes the information obtained in the interview is a good check on the accuracy of your recording and an excellent basis for the law firm's retainer. Finally, a reporting letter is crucial evidence, if an issue arises between the firm and your client who asks why the hell you have taken the action you did on his behalf.

The next chapter focuses on interviewing non-client witnesses, but here, as a part of following up, you will often need to gather information from secondary sources. This may involve interviewing other witnesses, obtaining police reports, searching databases, or carrying out other activities that will help to nail down information that may be important in the months, even years, to come, in the life of the legal action. Doing this job thoroughly and effectively initially will have a positive impact on your client's likelihood of success. You must determine what needs to be done to build the store of information to support your client's claim. Then, you must relentlessly follow up on those leads, carefully recording it all. This is vital.

No one can prescribe the particular follow-up steps to take, after a client interview; the circumstances in each case will vary. The best follow-up is "whatever it takes." You will also need to develop consistent methods to report the information, track the progress of the file, report to the client, and follow up on leads. All of this contributes to the legal team's ability to serve the needs of each client.

> **"You must determine what needs to be done to build the store of information to support your client's claim. Then you must relentlessly follow up on those leads, carefully recording it all."**

The final aspect of this area of discussion is the use of a client diary. Most often used in personal injury situations, it is frequently called a "pain diary." In it, the client tracks his recovery (or lack of it) to assist in keeping the law firm updated on this. Sometimes, this will consist of notations on a large calendar, keeping track of various appointments and recording how the client feels each day. I once asked an elderly client to keep such a diary. When I asked for her record a few months later, she brought in four thick notebooks filled to the margins with tiny, precise writing, in very light pencil. It was an excruciating ordeal to read through all the notations. (Tips to guide clients in keeping a diary are discussed a few paragraphs down.)

Journals or diaries can help ensure that your client does not lose track of how his injuries progress, particularly when discoveries or a trial may be years from the time of the accident. There are issues surrounding the use of journals, however, including the question of whether they will be considered privileged, for the purpose of the litigation. This can be important. Imagine your client, an optimistic person, writing this:

> *Woke up this morning feeling great. I'm so happy to be fully recovered from the accident.*

Now, imagine that your client suffered a relapse and wanted to take back those premature conclusions, yet the diary had to be disclosed to the opposing side. Whether the diary is privileged or not depends on the reason the client kept the record. If it was done for the purpose of obtaining legal advice, it would likely be considered privileged; if the client kept it to track his progress, out of personal interest in her medical situation, it would not likely be privileged.

If your client is asked, on discovery, about personal records he has kept, he must acknowledge the existence of the diaries. He will likely then be asked why he kept the diaries. The answer to this question is crucial. The "correct" answer is, "I kept the diaries to assist me in obtaining legal advice from my lawyer," assuming he wishes to advance a claim of privilege.

Let us return now to the potential drawback of too much information. A client who fills pages of notebooks or computer files for each day will create a massive processing nightmare, which will likely fall into your lap. Limiting the volume of information is a matter of self-preservation. You can assist your client by providing him with some tips about what information is important—and the quantity of information that will be helpful to your firm. Having commented on limiting your client's tendency to produce a Russian novel about his injuries, you must be certain that the client understands the need to be complete in recounting details about injuries. Rest assured that not commenting on a specific injury will be taken by the opposing lawyer as evidence that your client had no complaint regarding that injury on that day. If the complaint re-emerges three weeks later, that lawyer will argue that it must have been caused by some other incident.

As a final note, diaries can have a negative impact on a client's recovery from an injury. Health has a psychological component. That is not to say, "It's all in your mind," but having an attitude that one is on the way to a full recovery can help speed the recovery. Persistent pain can lead to depression, which can slow a client's recovery, which prolongs, even amplifies, the pain, in a depressing cycle. A *pain diary* contributes to a client focusing on the negative—how much pain he had each day, rather than the positive, how much better he is than last week. This is almost inevitable, because of the adversarial system that we function in, but counterproductive for your client's recovery.

The best thing that can happen for your client is for him to have a full recovery. Perhaps you can lessen the negative impact of keeping a diary by encouraging him to complete the task but to remain positive about his recovery, warning him about the danger of "wallowing" in negativity about the injuries or their effects without suggesting that he is the "wallowing" type.

1. What is the difference between probing and leading questions?

2. How can either/or questions be misleading?

3. What kind of questions are used in a funnel sequence?

CHAPTER EXERCISES

1. Appendix F lists some typical beginnings for open-ended questions. Write out five more to use when interviewing a client.

2. Consider the impact of conducting an interview using solely closed questions.

3. Your 43-year-old client wants to sue a ski school, because he seriously fractured his leg when skiing down an advanced skier slope after just one lesson.

   A. If you want to determine what your client learned in his first ski lesson, the following questions *could* be asked.

      a. Can you tell me what the first lesson consisted of? (open)

      b. Did they teach you how to snowplow in the first lesson? (closed)

      c. Did you learn how to turn or slow down in that lesson? (either/or)

      d. They couldn't have taught you much in half an hour. (leading)

      e. What on earth were you thinking? (judgmental)

      Which approach would work best in an initial interview?

   B. Let's say you want to elicit some information about the quality of instruction. Would you ask:

      a. What can you tell me about the quality of instruction in the class? (open)

      b. Did the instructor tell you how much teaching experience he had? (closed)

      c. Did the instructor seem to know what he was talking about or not? (either/or)

      d. I don't imagine they pay these instructors very much, do they? (leading)

      e. Were any of your instructors Swiss? (irrelevant)

C. Now you want to consider your client's injuries. Notice the differences among these:

    a. Tell me about your injuries. (open)

    b. Was it a clean break? (closed)

    c. Did you break the tibia or fibula? (either/or)

    d. It must have taken quite a while for the rescue team to arrive. (leading)

    e. Did you receive immediate treatment? It must have been very painful. Was the swelling the big problem? What do you think about skiing now? (multiple)

D. As a final example, you are trying to determine your client's wage loss.

    a. Tell me about your income loss? (open)

    b. What do you earn per hour? (closed)

    c. Do you get paid every two weeks or monthly? (either/or)

    d. Do you think this has cost you more than $2,000? (leading)

    e. This has been costly for you. (statement)

How will the phrasing of this question affect the information that you obtain?

E. In determining what type of question to ask, your objective and the stage in the interview are important considerations. I always encourage interviewers to lean toward questions that will elicit fresh information from the client, and avoid the tainting impact of questions that supply an anticipated answer or that telegraph content you want to hear.

CHAPTER 7

Interviewing Non-Client Witnesses

In Brief

*This chapter examines some of the unique considerations in-
volved in interviewing non-client witnesses, including issues
about interviewing children and interpreting their statements.
In some senses, the interviewing task with non-client witnesses is simplified; in others much more complex. Keeping in
mind the specific concerns of "independent" witnesses, while
using the skills you develop in interviewing clients, will improve your effectiveness in this forum.*

The majority of your interviews will likely be with clients of the law firm. However,
special issues will arise when you will need to interview a witness who is not a client.
Most will probably be "friendly" or supportive witnesses identified by your client as
best able to help with her claim. You might also be interviewing witnesses who are
independent or neutral, people who are not aligned with either side of the litigation
and have no interest in who succeeds. A further category is the adverse or hostile
witness—persons allied with the other side of the litigation—who may, in fact, be
unrepentantly antagonistic toward you or your client. The bulk of text over the next
few pages concerns your interviews with all non-client witnesses. But, to begin, the
focus is on the independent witness, perhaps the easiest to interview.

INDEPENDENT WITNESSES

With the independent witness, tactics that are better avoided with clients can actually enhance accuracy and facilitate the finding of fact. An independent witness does
not have anything "at stake" and, therefore, is likely to be less anxious. She is just

there to help out, so she will usually have dramatically reduced "litigation anxiety," compared with a witness who is also a litigant. Since an independent witness is not a client, she usually has a diminished motive to fabricate or enhance the evidence to support her "case." She is just altruistically cooperating with the legal system, with nothing invested in the outcome. However, just because she is independent doesn't mean she will be a good witness for your client. One of your tasks will be to determine what the independent witness knows that can hurt your client's case. Knowing which witnesses to call at trial or, more risky, what areas of questioning to avoid, is as important as determining what information is helpful to your client's position.

With an independent witness, you are doing what most closely approximates pure fact finding. Presumably, because a witness has no "axe to grind," she will be happy to help out. With the true independent witness, the only factor working against her cooperation is her having an unpleasant legal experience.

You can make the legal process, at least in terms of your involvement with the witness, a pleasant experience. You can use your personality to charm the witness, not to imply trying to get the witness to change her version of events, but simply to cheer her along in the process. An appropriate joke, a pleasant tone, appreciative comments that acknowledge that the witness is taking her valuable time to help out the process, are all ways to acknowledge the contribution made by the witness.

ALL NON-CLIENT WITNESSES

Planning

Planning your interview with a witness is very similar to planning a client interview. With a non-client witness, you will likely have a good idea, from speaking with your client, of what the witness may be able to tell you. Thus, you could start from the point of what you want, or need, to find out from the witness, using this to frame your interview. But you will have organized your thoughts, so you aren't rambling through the interview. This shows consideration for the witness's time—there is nothing more annoying to someone who's busy than dealing with a disorganized person.

Now, at the top of your plan, put three items: self-identify, atmosphere, connections. When you make your call—but before you launch into your questions—these tasks need attention.

Identifying Yourself

You must first tell the witness who you are, particularly your position in the firm. This most often arises when you are speaking with a witness by telephone. Witnesses, unfamiliar with the court process, often get confused about who is who. Words like plaintiff, defendant, applicant, respondent, and complainant can confound anyone unfamiliar with legal terminology. It is important for the witness to know "which side" of the litigation she is talking to. Although it really shouldn't

> "One of your tasks will be to determine what the independent witness knows that can hurt your client's case."

I recall an incident where I contacted a person who had given her name, address, and phone number to my client at the scene of an accident, but when I contacted her on my client's behalf, she adamantly denied any knowledge of the accident. She insisted she had never been there. I concluded that she was initially motivated by her social conscience to help out, and later, when she considered the inconvenience participation in the legal arena would present her, she got cold feet.

matter, a witness can—and will—feel abused or "ripped off" if she speaks openly with the interviewer, thinking he is acting for the other party.

This raises a related point. The witness, as with everyone you interview, must be aware that you are *not* a lawyer. This must be standard practice in all your dealings with the public.

Setting the Atmosphere

Check with the witness to see if it is a good time to talk—not at dinner time, or when she needs to put kids to bed—and thanking her for her time, perhaps pointing out the importance of getting this information from independent witnesses. You might also acknowledge the inconvenience or disruption this must be in her busy life, the anxiety that most people feel regarding dealing with the legal system, and the unpleasantness that accompanies dealing with pushy and insensitive lawyers. If the witness is required for trial, she may lose income, lose holiday time, or have to double up on her workload to catch up for time spent "cooling her heels," waiting to be called to testify. Looking at it from this perspective, why would anyone ever agree to be a witness? Oh, I forgot, we subpoena them so they have no choice—and that's something that's not apt to put a spring in her step.

Note: In spite of any comments implying that you will not take more of the witness's time than necessary, you must take as much time as necessary. Don't slip into leading (or helping) the witness to "save time." If you need to arrange another time to complete the interview, then do so, politely and respectfully.

Making Connections

You might need to—or just want to—cue the witness about the case, perhaps by referring to a specific aspect. This can help her remember the event *and* focus on your questions. In motor-vehicle-accident matters, for example, you might identify which car your client was in—the VW bug—or use some physical identifiers—the young woman with blonde hair, for example.

THE INTERVIEW: TACTICS AND PROCESS

One of the benefits of the interview process is that it happens outside the scrutiny of the judge or jury, so it is possible to fully explore the issues within the witness's knowledge, with nothing to lose. While you may not like what you hear—because it louses up the tidy little theory the firm has developed to represent your client—if you know the downside with respect to the evidence your client may be facing at trial, then the lawyer can properly assess the chances of success, perhaps putting heavy emphasis on the "s" word—settle.

The next issue is the care you must take in your manner of questioning non-client witnesses. As with your own client, the use of leading questions can corrupt evidence. An additional danger—with witnesses other than your client—is that you run the risk of embarrassing your law firm. The last thing the lawyer handling the matter wants to encounter in court is a witness, being cross-examined, looking awkwardly about and stating, "Well, I'm not sure if I should talk about that. The other lawyer told me I shouldn't mention that when testifying." The lawyer would be furious, and it could do irreparable harm to your client's case.

Of course, leading can be much more subtle, but there is no benefit to getting the witness to say one thing in the interview, only to have that witness (then being properly interviewed by the other side) provide a very different story on the stand.

> *Let's now imagine a variation on that car-crash scenario. As a result of the defendant smashing into your client's car in the intersection, your client has lost her job and is currently struggling to raise her three kids on welfare. None of that would have happened, of course, if the defendant had paid attention to the lights at the intersection. You also suspect he'd been drinking. Now, can you confirm that the defendant crashed into your client while running a red light? Also, given the above scenario, let's assume you have no evidence of drinking and that the information you have about the lights is ambiguous, at best.*

> **"There is no benefit to getting the witness to say one thing in the interview, only to have that witness (then being properly interviewed by the other side) provide a very different story on the stand."**

Various approaches can be used to encourage a witness to colour her evidence in your client's favour. You might try to get the witness to like your client—the struggling welfare mom. Conversely, you might try to show the other side in an unfavourable light, so the witness will dislike him—the intoxicated, reckless driver. Avoid these tactics. The witness's evidence can also be tainted by reviewing what other witnesses claim to have seen, thus encouraging this witness to adopt these observations or fill in the missing bits. Other techniques can be employed to cater to a witness's biases or predispositions. Using its lowest form, you could undermine the opponent through racial or sex stereotyping. Such actions should never be considered. They are not worthy of you; they will likely backfire; and they could certainly destroy the reputation of the law firm.

> **"Be sure to be accurate— faithful to what the client has told you. Don't over-shoot the mark by trying to have the witness say more than she has told you."**

While not leading the witness in your questioning of her is important, a more serious line is crossed by *misleading* a witness. This can happen intentionally or unintentionally. One way is by colouring the facts to enhance your client's version of events or her likeability.

Finally, if the information is valuable to your client, put it in writing. Either the witness can write out a statement, or you can write it out and send it to her for verification and signature. If you are writing it out, be accurate—faithful to what the witness has told you. Don't overshoot the mark by trying to have the witness say more than she has told you. Doing so can easily alienate the witness: she will feel manipulated, perhaps even betrayed, and that does not make for a good trial witness.

In the end, you want accurate and complete information from a witness who feels good about involvement with your law firm. And it just makes sense to help the witness feel appreciative of how she has been treated by you, when much of what the witness will say in court has a subjective element.

Keep in mind that what you are doing is reviewing the "facts"—as the witness recalls them—to determine what can or will become evidence. Decisions, either at trial or prior to trial, are based on the evidence, the information that will come before the judge or jury. The witness's facts may fit into this evidence category, or they may lead to other facts that will assist in clarifying matters, but any witness is a valuable resource and should be treated as such.

REALITY, MEMORY, AND "FACTS"

A philosopher might tell you that there is no such thing as reality. To illustrate, a famous philosophical question asks, "If a tree falls in the forest and no one is there, does it make any sound?" So the philosopher says, reality only has meaning in the context of each person's perception. Similarly, memory is a flexible concept. Two people experiencing the same events will often, even usually, describe significantly different experiences. (Setting aside the issue of fabrication, let us assume we are dealing solely with honest witnesses who want to help.) This is because memories are not like videotapes, they wax and wane, shift and fluctuate, based on the unique characteristics of the observer/listener at that unique moment. It is not possible to "freeze frame" an individual's memory so that minute details—perhaps ones that the person did not focus on at the time—can be studied. One way of viewing this is like the pieces of a puzzle. Where there are gaps, the picture may be unclear, and looking at a piece out of context may have little value in understanding the bigger picture. With memory, we rely on the flawed ability of a witness to reproduce her experience. However, it is simply the best we can do—with people.

All perception is based on an individual's personal perspective, which itself is an amalgam of:

- each person's mood and emotional state at the time of the experience,
- past experiences,
- biases or personal orientation,
- physical connection to the events, and
- a potential multitude of other factors.

For example, a man dressed in biker gear can arouse, in an observer, feelings of sexual excitement,

While representing a client who was rear-ended in a motor vehicle accident, I contacted a witness who had run to my client's car, after the accident, and observed him in a dazed state, with pattern marks on his forehead consistent with his head banging the steering wheel. At trial, the defendant claimed that the collision was so minimal that it would not result in any movement by the plaintiff (my client) inside his vehicle. The good Samaritan was therefore an important witness, and apparently willing, since she had provided my client with her card and had subsequently provided a general statement about the accident. For various reasons, I had been unable to actually speak to this witness until shortly before trial. When I finally spoke to her, she appeared distant, distrustful, and reluctant to help my client. I was puzzled by this, but it became clear that the lawyer for the defendant had spoken to her, and I could only conclude that something said by that lawyer had "put her off" my client. I suspect she had been led to conclude that my client was just a money grubber—which was far from the truth, by the way. But I still had to use her, since she could confirm that my client had been dazed and had this marking on his forehead. When I called her to testify, I asked her two substantive questions: "When you reached my client's car, how did he appear to you?" and "Did you notice any markings on the plaintiff?" She gave me the answers that I expected. She was not cross-examined. In this instance, I had to restrict my questioning very narrowly, since I could not trust the witness not to try to hurt my client's case. The wording of the questions carefully followed the responses from my earlier interview with her.

"So the philosopher says, reality only has meaning in the context of each person's perception."

in another exaggerated fear for his personal safety. These two reactions are not necessarily opposite: the sexual arousal may be connected to the "bad boy" sense of danger the biker represents. Nevertheless, depending on the observer's state of mind, the reconstructive process, after an incident, will vary greatly.

For one person, the biker may be remembered as acting decisively, but in a charming, seductive way. The other witness may have observed the same actions, but sees the leather-clad actor as a storm trooper—threatening, abusive, even vicious. People tend to remember those aspects that confirm their emotional predispositions, and they forget or glance over the ones that don't fit this mould. It is not just what may be selectively remembered; what is selectively forgotten also matters.

A factor that a witness dismisses and forgets can be crucial to a clear understanding of the event at issue. Proper interviewing can enhance accurate recall and can even help to fill in the blanks, reliably. Improper interviewing can result in inaccurate or additive recall. This is where something that did not happen is remembered by the witness, even an honest witness, who will adamantly insist that the events occurred precisely as she describes them. (Through some complex cognitive process, a witness can place a weapon in the hand of one of the individuals who were engaged in a violent episode. A weapon that, objectively, could not have been there.)

"It is not just what may be selectively remembered; what is selectively forgotten also matters."

Experienced trial lawyers are all too familiar with the frailties of eyewitness identification. (Again, this is not involving witnesses who are trying to distort.) These witnesses are trying their best to help out; they simply are notoriously unreliable. Even some judges, who you might presume would know better, can't bring themselves to believe that a witness's memory, or eyewitness identification, can be so unreliable. The myth of the reliability of memory is probably preserved because we are seldom in situations where our own ability to observe and reliably recall is objectively tested.

Our memories are tested when we write exams. Of course, those of us who do well in this forum are functioning in an "artificial" circumstance: we have had lots of notice, we know which facts we will be tested on, we have a controlled setting to record our answers, and the information we are to regurgitate remains stable. Additionally, there are usually no physical threats or danger present.

If we do not do well in these testing situations, we can dismiss its significance by pointing to the artificiality of the setting. We can assure ourselves that our memories of "real life" are far more accurate than our recollection of algebraic formulas or the lesser-known actors in the Bolshevik revolution.

Without any true test of our reliability, we assume an accuracy that does not stand up to objective assessment in controlled studies. Given the frailty of such witness accounts, how can we as interviewers enhance a witness's reliability?

FACTORS THAT ENHANCE/DIMINISH RELIABILITY

Reliability of a witness has three components: the ability to observe the event, recall what has been observed, and recount those observations on demand.

In considering the witness's ability to observe, several factors—some concerning the witness, some from the environment surrounding the incident—may affect this capacity. Regarding the witness, you must consider anything that would enhance or impair the witness's ability to observe. Does the witness wear glasses? Does she require a hearing aid? Was the witness drinking or taking prescription or non-prescription drugs? Was she tired, hungry, distracted? Has she suffered an injury, or is she in an abnormal mental state? One element of this is simply the individual's mental functioning. Some people have better memories than others and thus can be more precise, reliable witnesses. The passage of time affects witnesses differently: some people have the cramming-for-exams type of memory—they know everything in detail for a day or two, and then they purge their brains to let in new information. They are all but useless in recalling the "crammed" information a year and a half later. All of these factors must be considered in determining the value of a witness's observations. For example, the nearsighted witness who was not wearing corrective lenses, who positively identifies the accused from 60 feet away on a dark, moonless night, leaves something to be desired.

We also need to explore whether there are any factors that might cause the witness to be biased or inclined to modify her "facts" to help out one party or the other—or if the witness has any self-interest in the outcome. Whether a bias can help or hinder your client's case, the perception of bias is often as important as the reality. A perfectly good witness can be neutralized when being questioned by the other counsel—for example, if a previously undisclosed relationship with one of the parties to the litigation is unearthed. The lawyer presenting your client's case definitely does not want to hear about this for the first time when his star witness is in the stand.

> **"In considering the witness's ability to observe, several factors—some concerning the witness, some from the environment surrounding the incident—may affect this capacity."**

Now, we look at the environment surrounding the events in question. Was it a dark evening? If so, was there plenty of artificial illumination? How long did the witness observe the events? Was the witness in any danger at the time? Was there anything that obscured the witness's view or otherwise affected the quality of her observation? In questioning a witness, it is important to determine these "quality-of-observation" questions, since the party on the other side of the litigation is bound to do just that.

Consider eyewitness identification at a drive-by shooting incident. Questions you will want answered from the witness include the following:

- Where were you standing relative to the person shot and the shooter?

- Was anything obscuring your vision?

- At what point was your attention drawn to the event? (Just at the time of the gunfire or after hearing screeching tires half a block away?)

- What time of day was it?

- If at night, what was the natural light like?

- What was the artificial light like?

- What was the weather like?

- How fast was the vehicle travelling—and did it slow down or speed up at any point?

- Was the shooter inside the car? (Did the shooter get out of the car, hang out of the car?)

- Describe the vehicle. Was anything (tinted windows) obscuring your vision?

- How long did the whole incident take?

- What were you doing immediately prior to the incident?

In a similar incident, these questions would not necessarily be asked in that order or in the manner shown, but they represent things you would want to know about the circumstances and the environment surrounding the observations. There are, of course many more aspects to be explored.

This doesn't mean that you pepper the witness with a string of closed questions. You should encourage her to provide her version of events, holding back your narrow or leading questions. Just remember that there are a huge number of factors that affect the quality of your witness's observations, and by the end of the interview you should be knowledgeable in relation to those factors.

> **"There are a huge number of factors that affect the quality of your witness's observations, and by the end of the interview you should be aware of those factors."**

Another aspect to consider is witness contamination. The problem here cannot be stressed enough—it has the potential to distort the information provided. Witnesses will, at times, be telling you things that they could not possibly have experienced. It is helpful to know whom the witness has talked to, why the witness has done so, and what she learned from that source. When witnesses "share" information, evidence can get homogenized, and that may undo the value of what your witness may have been able to offer.

Another element in assessing your witness's ability to assist your client's case, is her ability to communicate. Some potential witnesses do not present well. They seem shifty and evasive for no objective reason. Or sometimes, either through nervousness, lack of sophistication, or limited intelligence, witnesses have difficulty communicating what they may know very well. As you interview your witness, you should be assessing her value in the witness stand. If you conclude that her value is marginal or even negative, pass that on to the lawyer. Few lawyers throw whatever witnesses they have at the court, regardless of how they come across.

So, in conducting your interview, you are not only gathering information but assessing the witness for reliability and her potential impact on a judge or jury. Keep your receptors tuned for all these components.

Let's imagine that your law firm is representing a person who has been involved in an automobile collision. Your client was seriously injured, in fact suffered from a concussion and has little memory of the events of the night in question. The police report indicates that there is a witness who was driving by in a car that was not involved in the accident. You contact the witness and set up an appointment to interview her. So, you need to find out as much as you can about the cause of the accident. How do you then begin?

Let's start with how not to begin. Do not ask the witness to tell you who caused the accident. This "backward" approach immediately invites the witness to draw a conclusion, a conclusion, by the way, that may not favour your client. The witness may then be inclined to selectively remember information that supports the conclusion she has already come to—not a good place to start in getting at the facts.

Rather, you should structure the interview to help the witness revisit the circumstances of the accident in a manner that will increase the likelihood of her remembering important details. Start before the accident, perhaps where was the witness was coming from that day. Naturally, the witness should be invited to describe the incident, providing as much detail as possible. You will be interested in her information, but also in the value of this witness. How reliable is the information she provides you? How effective will she be, if your client needs her information in court? Consider the following matters. What had she been doing before the accident? Was she familiar with the route? What were the road conditions? Was anything distracting her from focusing on the road? What about lighting, weather, traffic, and any other factors that might affect the witness's ability to "take in" what happened?

Now, direct your witness to the time immediately prior to the accident. When did she first notice either car? What was the position of the cars at that time? Did she notice anything about the driving of (movement of) either car? Did she notice the colour of the traffic lights? Basically, you want to discover the factors of causation, without the witness being pressed for a conclusion on that point.

After all, it is not particularly important who the witness thinks is at fault. What will matter is the quality of the evidence put before the judge or jury on that point. You must be sure that the witness has exhausted her memory and that you know the impediments or problems that this witness faced at the time of the accident.

> **"So, in conducting your interview, you are not only gathering information but assessing the witness for reliability and her potential impact on a judge or jury. Keep your receptors tuned for all these components."**

Two final points need attention regarding the reliability of witness statements. Studies have shown that so-called professional witnesses, such as police officers, suffer from the same lapses as lay witnesses in their judgment biases and tendencies to fill in the blanks in their memories. You must keep this in mind, whether you are preparing professional witnesses or preparing other witnesses to challenge such "expert" testimony.

The other cautionary point is that the confidence expressed by the witness regarding her own testimony is no indicator of its reliability. Witnesses who have gotten it very wrong are often the most sure that they have it 100 percent right, whereas the cautious witness may be the most realistic and, in fact, the most accurate. So, when working with any witness, approach their evidence with healthy skepticism, recognizing the strengths and weaknesses in the information they present.

SECOND-LANGUAGE INTERPRETATION

With greater and greater numbers of people moving about the world, it is common for law firms to be dealing with individuals whose English-language capabilities are limited. For some, the limitations are extreme and can only be addressed through the assistance of an interpreter. For others, it is possible to conduct the interview without interpretation; however, great care must be exercised to ensure that you understand the information you are receiving, exactly—and that the questions you ask are comprehended accurately.

Never has the use of plain language been as important as when interviewing a person whose native language is not English. In the context of an interview, one of the valuable purposes of small talk is that it permits you to assess the interviewee's command of English and to adjust your strategies accordingly. Try to avoid insulting the client by using language that is too elementary; at the same time, if you use legalisms and unfamiliar idioms, meaningful participation from the interviewee will be lost. Similarly, much of the content you communicate may elude the interviewee, if she is searching her memory for the meaning of "mitigate," "frustrate," "contingent"—and expressions like "Catch 22," "a stitch in time," "topping up," and "go for the gold." Words or expressions taken for granted by many of us in everyday usage may leave witnesses or clients in the dark. A few further examples, with simplified alternative words, are shown below.

fractured	broken
subsequent to	after
tentative	uncertain
distill	reduce
cumulative	total
contemplate	think
liken	compare
withhold	keep
acquire	get

Can you simplify the following sentence?

> *Simon posited a radically reduced temporal component to the contractual obligations.*

Or,

> *Dirk will require an extension of the specified deadline, so as to facilitate his analysis of the varying components of the proposal and formulate a decisive response.*

Plain-language communication is also valuable when working with clients for whom English is *not* a challenge. Use of clear and simple language is usually an indication of clarity of thought. This is one more reason why pacing your interview, to allow you to formulate a good question before you ask it, is a valuable practice.

Interpreters

With someone whose ability in English is severely limited, an interpreter is essential. The quality of the interview, in this instance, will thus depend on both the quality of your questioning and the professional ability of the interpreter. The expression "Something was lost in translation" has its origins in real situations.

Having a relative or family friend as an interpreter can save your witness or client money, but may result in a loss of content, and that is not acceptable. In addition, not all family or friends are neutral, as one would expect the professional interpreter to be, and there is the danger of a relative interpreting *and* "putting his own spin" on the facts. The interviewee may well feel influenced or intimidated in the presence of a relative, particularly when "the truth" of the situation does not cast her in a positive light.

When working with a professional interpreter, you should satisfy yourself that he shares your understanding of his role in the process. What is essential is that the interpreter does *not* see his role as *interpreting* your questions or *interpreting* the answers from the perspective of translating what he thinks the individual really meant to say. The actual words spoken are essential, although a good interpreter will stop and seek clarity if he thinks the intended meaning is being lost. It is then possible to sort that out on the spot, rather than having the miscommunication lost within a long interview. The interpreter must not summarize or redefine your questions to the client. This could leave out important details and result in a very different question than the one you asked being answered. Likewise, he must not abbreviate or synthesize the interviewee's answers. He must not indicate what the witness/client intended to say, except to the extent referred to above, where he indicates that further inquiry might help to sort through a potential misunderstanding.

Keep in mind that interpretation is not a precise science. Some consider it to be more art than science, given the subtleties of communicating across cultures. There are so many ways that this process can go wrong that I strongly urge you to work with professionals, particularly ones who you know will operate on an agreed set of rules and who will not cut corners to shorten what is often a lengthy and exhaustive process. Be considerate of the fact that the interpreter is performing a very complex mental process and will tire from that. Be sure to give him a break before the quality of his interpretation breaks down.

At a hearing, I represented a client who was making a refugee claim. The essence of the claim was that my client had a well-founded fear of persecution if returned to his country. In describing the mistreatment he received from the authorities in his country of origin, my client was describing an interview he had with the police. The interpreter, at the hearing, stated that the authorities treated him with *extreme prejudice*.

There was a bit of a commotion among two of his supporters, who were in the hearing room, and I leaned back to see what their concern was. They informed me that what my client had actually said was that the police *tortured* him. I suggested to the hearing that the interpreter had translated the words incorrectly. The interpreter acknowledged that what my client said *could be interpreted as tortured*, but *extreme prejudice* was also an acceptable translation.

My client went on to describe the treatment, which included severe and repeated beatings and the application of electric shocks to his genitals. After that, I believe that everyone in the room, with perhaps the exception of the interpreter, considered that the word *torture* was a more apt description than the expression *extreme prejudice*.

Winston Sayson, who is both a prosecutor and a parent, tells a story of an incident with his own young child. Sayson heard his son in the bathroom and distinctly heard the sound of keys clinking in the toilet bowl and then the toilet being flushed. Sayson rushed into the room and confronted his child about flushing the keys down the toilet. His son repeatedly denied the allegation, but with the persistence and skill of a trained prosecutor, Winston finally managed to get the child to admit that he had, in fact, flushed the keys down the toilet. The child said, "I'm sorry I flushed your keys down the toilet." All well and good in the pursuit of truth and justice—except for one fact. The next day, Sayson found his keys in the corner on the tile floor of the bathroom. The sound of keys hitting the tiles is remarkably similar to the sound of them hitting the toilet bowl. Yet the child succumbed to the persistent interrogation and admitted to an offence he had not committed.

"As with all of us, attentive and thoughtful listening will go a long way to establishing rapport with a child of any age."

INTERVIEWING CHILDREN

Interviewing children is a challenging task. However, it is possible to over-emphasize the uniqueness of this particular type of interview. But if you apply the principles of good interviewing with *any* witness, you will be well set up to conduct an interview of a child.

Professionals are perhaps most concerned with the dangerous effect of leading questions when interviewing children. Children are seen as easily swayed and, therefore, suggesting an answer through a leading question has the danger of supplying inaccurate information that a child may confirm. For the purpose of testifying in court, a person under the age of 14 is considered a child, and special rules apply in dealing with child testimony. So it could even be misleading to lump all children into one group for the purpose of considering how to conduct interviews with them.

A child being interviewed could be 3 or 14 years old, and the level of sophistication and cooperation one would expect between those two ages varies enormously. The younger the child, the more supportive and empathetic you will need to be. As a child approaches the teen years, it may be important for that support to transform into respect and acceptance.

Those who are familiar with younger and older children would challenge the proposition that older children are more confident and have less need for empathic understanding than the very young. In my experience with teenaged children, they seem to react quickly and negatively to any hint that adults are treating them in a patronizing manner. As with all of us, attentive and thoughtful listening will go a long way to establishing rapport with a child of any age.

While there are some general rules to consider, you will have to make your own assessment of where any *particular* child lies on the continuum of maturity—and modify your interviewing style accordingly.

When interviewing children, one factor does need special consideration: the potential distorting impact of previous interviews on the same topic by other people. As already discussed, all witnesses are susceptible to the suggestive impact of leading questions. No matter how "good" you are by not asking any leading questions, if the previous interviewer has supplied answers over and over, children may adopt the answers as their own.

Remember that previous interviewers may have been relatives, even parents, and a child may be quite influenced by this adult's perception of reality. Since you were not there for the earlier interviews, you can't control that process. What you can do is determine whether the child has previously been interviewed, by whom, and how often. You may even be in a position to attempt to "recover data." You do this by asking the child to go back to before their interview(s) with others and to take a fresh look at the incident. The success of this approach will largely depend on the time that has passed since the incident in issue, the point at which the other interview took place, and the degree to which the child has adopted the supplied version as his own. The child may be able to supply information about the previous interviews that will be of assistance. It is at least worth asking.

> *What did you talk about with your uncle when he spoke with you?*
>
> We talked about my mommy's boyfriend, Pete.
>
> *Do you recall what your uncle said to you?*
>
> He was asking about whether Pete is mean to me.
>
> *Anything else that you remember?*
>
> Yeah, I remember telling Uncle Sid that Pete takes me to lots of neat places and helps me with my homework.
>
> *Anything else?*
>
> Well … Uncle Sid said that Pete is a mean man and asked me whether he ever hurt me.
>
> *And what did you tell your Uncle Sid?*
>
> I … I … I said no, but he seemed to get real mad at me … and so I told him I guess so, and it was all right after that.
>
> *You told your Uncle Sid that Pete hurt you?*
>
> Yes … I guess so.
>
> *And did Pete ever hurt you?*
>
> No … Pete's really nice, he wouldn't do that.
>
> *Do you feel OK talking to me about this?*
>
> Am I going to get in trouble for saying Pete did something and he didn't?
>
> *You should always tell the truth, and no one can get you in trouble then. OK?*
>
> OK.

What you are attempting to do is look for contamination of the evidence, not add to it. In dealing with a child, it can be quite difficult when there are overlays of bad interviewing to cut through.

In your initial contact with the child, you can ask some relatively innocuous questions, and the answers may tell you a great deal about how the child has been prepared for the interview. If you approach the issue too directly, you may get a programmed answer, but the child's answer to an indirect question might tell you a lot.

*Hi, Tony, my name is Barbara Topping, I work at the law firm. Every-
one calls me Babs. Is that all right with you?*

Yeah, that's fine.

Can I get you anything before we start, a pop or a cookie?

No … thank you.

Babs. It's OK to call me Babs.

OK. Babs … [giggle]

All right Tony [giggle], can you tell me why you are here today?

Mom said it was about the bad man in the park.

Fine, let's start there. What can you tell me about the man?

He's bad.

Yes, you said that. Can you tell me why you think he is bad?

Mom said he hurts little kids.

What do you know about the man? I'd like to hear that.

Mom said he comes to the park to bother the kids.

Have you ever seen him bothering children?

No … but Mom said …

Has he ever bothered you?

I don't think so, I've never seen him.

I once prosecuted a person for threatening two of his neighbours. On the day of the trial, the defence lawyer indicated that he was going to call the accused man's child to testify about the events on the day in question. On a break before the case was called in court, I saw the defence lawyer talking to the child in the hallway. He was saying, quite loudly, "You be sure to tell the truth … or else I'm going to give you a big smack." The lawyer probably thought he was being humorous, and I suspect he said this for my benefit—to confirm that he had told the child to tell the truth. I was concerned about the child's dad's lawyer telling this child, who lived with this pretty scary guy, that he was going to get a big smack.

Obviously there are many unanswered questions, but you have some sense of where Tony got most of his information.

It is also helpful to know how any particular child relates to adults or authority figures. This may tell you something about what impact the earlier interviews may have had on the child, but it may also tell you something about how the child is relating to you in the interview. For example, a child who comes from a background where questioning adults brings punishment is unlikely to correct mistakes in your understanding of the events.

You may never get to know the child well enough to eliminate all of the possible "contaminants" to the information provided, but you can be alert to the prospect. One way is simply to get to know the child a little. There are significant benefits to this approach. I heard one prosecutor say that, time permitting, he doesn't go into the details of sexual assault allegations with young children until the third meeting. Obviously, you can't do this with every interview for every child, but be aware that the better you know a child, the more free he or she will feel in discussing matters openly with you. You could try the old, "How about an ice cream cone?" approach, or a little change of scenery, and then ease into the discussion. By the way, this would not be a helpful approach if the child is particularly suspicious of strangers offering gifts. It may help if a parent or trusted adult is present, but be careful of that person's influence over what the child says. Talk to the adult separately, making sure that she or he knows not to answer for the child or in any other way influence the answers. Answers must always be the child's—or there is no point to the interview.

> **"A child who comes from a background where questioning adults brings punishment is unlikely to correct mistakes in your understanding of the events."**

There was a notorious case involving allegations of ritual physical and sexual abuse of children. Charges were brought against a number of adults associated with a daycare centre. The police decided to bring in an expert to interview the children. The problem was that the "expert" had completely inflated her qualifications, and she approached the entire process from the perspective that the children had been horribly abused and that she was going to "get it out of them."

Fortunately, for the defendants, these interviews were videotaped, which allowed the court to view the atrocious corruption of the evidence from the child witnesses by the "expert." In one scene, she asked a child whether one of the workers had ever touched him sexually. He clearly and emphatically said the worker hadn't. She became quite insistent, going so far as to tell the child that other children had remembered the abuse and insisting that he must be very stupid to have forgotten. Her questions at this point became badgering, along the lines of "Are you stupid? Are you a stupid boy?" At this, the child finally broke down and agreed that he also remembered the abuse. He was then told what a good boy he was.

Unfortunately and too often, there is no record of the method used in questioning a child, and one is left to sort through the remnants of those conversations within the child's memory.

When speaking to children, try to cast your mind back, through the dark reaches of time, to when you were a child being *talked to* by an adult. Such conversations are often among the most uncomfortable experiences for children. Depending on the child, his non-parent adult contact often might consist of scolding or discipline situations. This is not a good set-up for your interview. You must speak to the child at his level, without legal jargon or other "big" words. But don't try to be too "cool." Children are likely to think you are just weird.

A legal interview is intimidating for most children. It may, in fact, be scary. Telling a child, "There's nothing to be scared of" is just silly. No one in the history of the universe ever stopped feeling scared because someone told them that there is nothing to be scared of. What about, "It's a bit scary, isn't it? Well, I've done this lots of times before, and we will get through it fine." Say something to assure the child, without belittling his apprehension.

"Telling a child, 'There's nothing to be scared of' is just silly. No one in the history of the universe ever stopped feeling scared because someone told them that there is nothing to be scared of."

As with all witnesses, ask clear questions. The question that meanders all over the map, until it finally comes to rest on one particular point, will frustrate—or just bewilder—a child. Always avoid multiple questions. Use open questions, but remember these need not be, "So how's it going?" You can direct the child to what you need to know: "Tell me about the fight that you saw last Tuesday."

Do not express *any* judgmental thoughts when interviewing a child. If something that he is telling you does not add up, you can tell the child, without implying that he is lying, "Now, Dustin, I need you to help me with something. You told me that the first time your Uncle Fred touched you was on Christmas Eve last year, but your mom told me that Uncle Fred didn't get home until the day after Christmas. Can you help me figure that out?" It should be obvious that you wouldn't say to a child, "Why would you go in the car with a stranger?" First, you don't want to shift the blame to the victim, but more important, for the pursuit of information, the child will immediately close down and you might as well go home. Why would the child risk further criticism, when shutting up doesn't give you anything to attack?

Children are a special sort of non-client witness, but by treating them with the same care and respect with which you treat client witnesses, you will enhance the quality of the information they provide.

CHAPTER QUESTIONS

1. Outline the similarities and differences in interview situations involving clients and independent witnesses.

2. Is eyewitness testimony the most reliable form of evidence? Why?

3. What special considerations exist in interviewing witnesses who do not speak English well?

4. State three factors that are important when interviewing children.

CHAPTER EXERCISES

1. Find someone who will trust you to interview their child. Get their permission. Then conduct an interview with the child. It need not be about a legal matter, but try to find something that might give you a bit of a challenge and be interesting for the child. Perhaps the child did observe something that might go to court, like a car accident. Or you could speak to her about bullying in schools. Perhaps have the child describe an incident or person within her experience. Look for something where detail and accuracy may be important. Do the interview. Ask the child how you did in the interview. Evaluate your performance. What could you, would you, do differently in the future.

2. Talk with someone who is in the process of learning English. Pay attention to her construction or reconstruction of English, the turns of phrases, and the necessary contortions needed in trying to communicate with limited vocabulary and grammar. Consider the modifications in your communication style that you undergo in trying to be understood in this circumstance. Don't raise your voice in order to be understood better. While it may surprise some people, English doesn't actually get any easier to understand at higher decibels.

CHAPTER 8

Client Advice, Ethical Concerns, and Troublesome Clients

In Brief

This chapter reviews a number of special considerations for the interviewer, from the concern about giving legal advice to ethical challenges and conflicts of interest. There are also suggestions for how to approach interviewing a variety of "difficult" clients.

DRESS FOR SUCCESS

Appearance matters—to your clients and to members of your law office. You will have your own style, but the firm you work with will often have a say in the staff's style of dress.

Many firms have casual Fridays. That aside, put some thought into how you dress; it influences different clients differently. Formal attire may be either expected as a sign of professionalism or intimidating to clients. Very casual attire may be distracting or, for some clients, a sign of sloppy work. As with other aspects of interviewing, make a conscious decision about the atmosphere you create through your style of dress.

LIMITATIONS ON YOUR "ADVICE"

You are not a lawyer. This is hugely important, because many people using the services of a law firm will not make a distinction about what training or legal background any staff member has.

"What you tell clients will, almost certainly, be attributed to the lawyer acting on the file."

When I first became a lawyer, friends and acquaintances would stop me and raise a legal issue they were involved with, asking my advice. My wife would often preempt me with a commonsense answer. Having spent four years at law school, plus articling, I took some exception to this casual approach to my vocation. My friends were following the legal advice of a drama teacher. This might work in auditions for theatre companies, but I wouldn't rely on it to keep me out of jail or to make a decision to sue or defend an action.

The big problem for me was that her advice would undoubtedly be attributed to me, in that strange process by which married couples become associated. You will have a similar association with a large and confusing machine of the law firm, and what you tell a client will, almost certainly, be attributed to the lawyer acting on the file. The lawyer will not be present for most of your dealings with clients; therefore, she will be unable to consider the statements with care and ensure that subtle nuances are not lost on the client. But when the lawyer is absent, she has accountability without control—not something lawyers like.

Let's try out a few examples. On a house transfer, a client asks you what the difference is between joint tenancy and tenants in common. You state that "joint tenants receive the other person's share of the property if that person dies, whereas, with tenants in common, the deceased person's share of the property goes into his own estate." This is a reasonable description; however, depending on the circumstance, it might be appropriate to tell the client that when a property is put in joint tenancy, the joint tenant relationship can be severed, so that it transforms into a tenants in common situation. This can be done by either party at any time.

Another example may be with drafting a will. You might tell a couple who are engaged to be married that "marriage will invalidate a will that exists before the marriage date." Perhaps, in the circumstances, you should have informed your clients that they can enter into a will "in contemplation" of marriage and it won't be invalidated, or that the wills they are signing contain a provision that all former wills are revoked. And if this will is invalidated, the former wills remain revoked, so the person may die intestate, without any will. The appropriateness of this advice will depend on the circumstances, and the decision about whether advice is needed, and to what extent, is one for the lawyer to make. All those years of study have a value.

What sorts of things can you deal with, then? This is a difficult area to define, but it is an area that should be carefully clarified with the responsible lawyer. Some basic responses to simple procedural questions may be answered, but even those could result in a client being misinformed if the issue develops differently than anticipated. Keeping in mind the ethical limits imposed on lawyers, you will need to clearly establish, with your law firm, how much information you can provide. Some law firms allow their non-legal professionals to deal with clients on matters involving retainer agreements. I am definitely against this. A retainer agreement is a contract between the firm and the client, and it should be dealt with between the lawyer and the client directly.

You can, for example, discuss the various steps that take place in litigation, filing a statement of claim, examinations for discovery, and the like, but you should not suggest a particular strategy, "cleaning out the joint safe deposit box," or "changing the locks on the apartment," as these strategies will have long-term effects on the litigation. If you suggest a particular approach to a client and it differs from what the lawyer advises, the client will conclude at best, that the law firm isn't very coordinated in its representation; at worst, the client may prefer your approach, thus driving a wedge between you and the lawyer. The relationship might survive this one time, but twice would be pushing it. Questions from clients seeking legal advice *must* be referred to the lawyer.

> Can you tell me what my chances of winning would be?

> How should I go about notifying the tenants?

> What's the best time to commence such an action?

> Do I have to name my mother-in-law in the writ?

> How much will this cost me?

One thing no lawyer wants to hear is, "But your legal assistant said that … ." It would be even worse, if you are right and the lawyer wrong.

You should acknowledge the question and assure the client that you will bring it to the lawyer's attention and that she will respond to it as soon as possible. This is a perfect opportunity to practise "positive phrasing." What this means is how to say "no" to the client, without it seeming like you are refusing to help. Rather than saying "I can't help you with that question," you should consider how you might phrase this more positively. Neither would I recommend saying, "I'm not allowed to answer those kinds of questions." The latter answer might be interpreted as, "I really *do* know the answer, but these stupid rules stop me from helping." This may be good for your ego, but it is not good for the image the client has of the legal profession, or your firm in particular. Try a more positive "spin":

> *That's an excellent question. I'm going to make a note of it and bring it*
> *to the attention of the lawyer, Ms. Lal, so she can address this concern*
> *when you meet with her on Tuesday.*

You have "rewarded" the client for asking a good question, informed him when the matter will be addressed, and packaged it up, as if waiting until Tuesday to deal with it is a good thing. Law offices are in the service industry, and ensuring that our clients have a positive feeling about the service they receive is very important.

There is one piece of "legal advice" that you should be encouraged to give to clients. Consider the situation where you know—or suspect—that a client is about to take some step that could affect his legal rights or the progress of the litigation. This often happens with a client who is prone to "self-help" solutions.

> I oughta just go right over there and give that guy a piece of my mind.

> Perhaps I'll just write a brief note to explain … .

> The police officer left a voice mail. What do I say when I call him back?

The "legal advice" you should give to the client is, "Don't do anything until you have spoken with the lawyer." By recognizing the danger of the client acting on his own—and quite possibly jeopardizing his entire case—and by firmly dissuading him from taking any action without proper legal advice, you have provided a valuable service to your client.

That's not to say that clients should never take any action on their own behalf. Many "legal problems" can be resolved simply and quickly by a client taking an obvious step to resolve matters. However, because clients are generally too close to the problem, they should not take those steps until they have checked them out with a lawyer. It is just too easy to miss the obvious downside to the "self-help" solution, which may have serious consequences.

ETHICAL CHALLENGES

Within the context of a law office, non-lawyers have specified limits to their decision-making authority, so ethical challenges may not arise as frequently as they do for lawyers in the firm. Nevertheless, questions arise. The issues may range from a client asking you to change the date on a document, in order to assist him with an income tax problem, to a client seeking help in circumventing human rights legislation, so he can evict some tenants from his apartment building. In all instances, the most important task for you is to hone your skills at recognizing ethical issues. You might be surprised how often lawyers are disciplined for matters where they simply missed an ethical or conflict issue.

The law firm's relationship with a client is very private, but the representation of the client is most often very public. Law firms are held to a high level of scrutiny and must present an unimpeachable moral image. More than most other professions, lawyers must not only do the right thing but be seen to do the right thing. Since you are a front-line worker, you will often be the first to deal with ethical issues. So, you must be prepared to respond decisively to any dilemma presented by a client; otherwise, fairly or not, your firm may get the image of being "fuzzy" on ethical issues.

"Law firms are held to a high level of scrutiny and must present an unimpeachable moral image."

I have had clients whom I have represented on criminal charges on legal aid. Sometimes one of these clients will tell me something like, "If you do a good job for me I will pay you extra." This comment has a number of dimensions. First, it is insulting; it insinuates that I won't do a good job for the legal aid client unless I receive extra payment. Second, why is this person on legal aid, if he has funds that could be devoted to his legal representation? Third, the client, facing criminal charges, is asking the lawyer to conspire to defraud the legal aid system. The way to deal with this suggestion is to tell the client, firmly, that you would never consider this proposal. It is, at best, a civil fraud—at worst, a criminal offence. End of discussion. Anyone working for me would disabuse the client of this notion just as firmly and quickly.

As stated earlier, the first key to ethical problems is to recognize them. The next step is to inform the client, politely and firmly, that the law firm will not be involved in anything unethical. I say "politely," since a client can innocently make the suggestion, not realizing that it is unethical. Law firms operate under strict rules, and some clients are naive in dealing with social or business matters. This approach may seem stodgy to some, but law firms must happily run the risk of appearing quaint or "square" in their dealings with the world.

Some ethical issues need to be dealt with by your firm's lawyers; however, it is important for you to determine the firm's position on common problems ahead of time. If your client presents an ethical problem, and you indicate that the lawyer will get back to him on it, the appearance is left that the lawyer will think about it. In many instances, the damage to the firm's reputation has been done as soon as the client thinks that the lawyer *may* go along with an unethical suggestion.

Conflicts of Interest

Here's a concept that many people, including lawyers, find difficult to grasp. The law firm can't act for one client when that person's legal interests would conflict with another client's interests—or the lawyer's or the law firm's interests. Since law firms must adhere to the highest standards, even the appearance of a conflict is as deadly as its existence.

Conflicts should be avoided at all costs. Classic examples involve working for two partners in a business. It's all well and good when things are going smoothly, but what happens when the relationship breaks down? One partner is sure to ask why you didn't properly protect them when the business was set up (even if the law firm did everything it should have done). A huge potential exists for the spreading of bad feelings from disgruntled former clients. Married couples present a similar risk.

It is, of course, not your decision about representing a client or determining if a conflict or apparent conflict exists. However, since you will be working so intimately with the file, you may come to recognize a conflict of interest— or a potential for one—long before the lawyer would. To protect the firm, you should bring this matter to the lawyer's attention right away.

Confidentiality

The first duty of a lawyer is to protect the secrets of the client. The wartime navy's expression was, "Loose lips sink ships." Some clients have newsmaking litigation, attracting media attention, with reporters calling and television cameras parked outside the courthouse or even your law offices. It's tempting to share this information with a close friend, a spouse, your mother who lives in Timbuktu. Alert! Alert! Danger! Don't do it—ever. If you reveal client secrets, your career is only the first thing you will lose.

First and foremost, clients deserve confidentiality. They deserve to have absolute confidence that what they reveal, in getting legal representation, will stay within the walls of

I have a huge fish tank in my office. It would be even more impressive if I ever found the time to stock it with fish. I got the tank quite cheaply from a glass shop whose owner told me that he had made the tank for a seafood restaurant, but its owner never paid him for it. After numerous and frustrating demands for payment, the tank's maker went to the restaurant during its busy lunch hour and demanded payment. When he was rebuffed once again, he took a hammer from his tool kit and told the owner that unless the tank was returned right away, he would smash it on the spot. He got the tank back then and there. For him, this approach was preferable to lengthy and expensive litigation. Now, I would never advise a client to take such an action. He broke a number of laws and could easily have ended up "cooling his heels" in jail. But there are often solutions to problems that do not entail marching lock-step through the legal system. Lawyers should recognize those situations and advise clients, when they can, about other legal solutions that are not litigious, like mediation or negotiation.

the firm. Lawyers are very highly paid to provide the highest level of professionalism. To betray this confidence deserves the highest censure. Expect that this is what will happen if you break this trust.

Anything your client tells you that is in furtherance of litigation is privileged. Only the client can give you permission to talk about him or his "secrets." This means that you can't be subpoenaed to testify against a client of your firm. An exception to the privilege "rule" is that the advice cannot be for the purpose of aiding in the commission of an offence.

What constitutes a client's secret? Everything, even whether your firm is representing a particular client is secret, unless or until it becomes public knowledge. It might be titillating to tell your friends that your firm represents "the Vancouver Slasher," but he hasn't been formally charged, and if your secret reaches the wrong ears, your firm might well be looking at the wrong end of a lawsuit.

People may call and ask if you are representing a particular client. Find out who they are and why they are asking and get a number. The only way to be sure that it's OK to reveal the information is to get permission from the client. Most law firms want such permission in writing. Strangely enough, clients have been known to remember telephone conversations differently than law firm personnel do. C.Y.A.—cover your ass—is the best advice.

TROUBLESOME CLIENTS

This section offers some insights in dealing with various kinds of "difficult" clients. While most clients are fairly "average" people—motivated to work with you to reach a solution to the legal concerns facing them—law offices seem to be a magnet for unusual characters, many of whom are somewhat socially challenged. Some of this can be explained by the stress that accompanies legal issues; however, some clients are in legal messes precisely because of their peculiar behaviour. It might be nice to be able to pick and choose clients, but remember the colourful ones can actually add a little spice to your day, not entirely a bad thing in itself. What is important is that the troublesome aspects of a client not impair your ability to give him good representation. Let's look at some different types of clients and consider how they might be accommodated.

Hostile Clients

Starting with the hostile category doesn't imply that this is the most common type of difficult client you will encounter. However, it is not unusual for law firms to have hostile clients. This may strike you as odd; after all, the whole reason for a law firm to exist is to help clients resolve legal issues. But somehow,

I once reviewed a mortgage document that the bank required my client's wife to sign. She asked me to represent her and give a certificate of independent legal advice regarding a loan for my client's business that would be secured by a mortgage on their house. I pointed out the possible conflict to my client, the husband, before agreeing to represent his wife. He insisted I go ahead. I knew, given his circumstances, that I might advise his wife against signing the document. When I looked at the document, I could not, in fact, advise my client's wife to sign it. I told her so in no uncertain terms even though the husband's business was on shaky ground, and if his wife didn't sign, the bank had made it perfectly clear they would close him down. His wife signed the document against my advice; the business failed; and the bank seized both the business and their house. From my perspective, I avoided a conflict of interest by getting my client's permission (they couldn't afford to pay another firm for this advice) to act for his wife in this matter. I discharged my responsibility to her by advising her of the dangers of signing the bank's document. Frankly, it would have been much better for my client's wife to have received advice from another law firm. I am sure that they would have given her the same advice, but there would have been a greater appearance of independence.

some clients connect the law firm with the distressing and often unfair circumstances in their lives.

Legal conflict can throw normally stable people completely off balance and cause them to lash out at those people close to them, including their lawyers (and support staff). Clients prone to paranoia can suspect that the law firm is dragging their misery out in order to cash in on their suffering. There is some truth to the point that law firms profit from the unhappy circumstances of their clients. Legal representation *is* expensive; so, the more you are in a client's life, the more it costs him. Many clients, therefore, hear the meter ticking whenever they are dealing with you.

Typically, the hostile client is someone with a chip on his shoulder: he is looking for an argument, for one more unpleasant thing to happen to him. Everything that can be interpreted negatively will be, and the hostile client is not hesitant to let his feelings be known to you. In some instances, hostile clients are like little lambs when they deal with the lawyer, but they feel free to stomp on the support staff, as a way of venting their frustration. Let's try an interview with a hostile client.

> *Good morning, Mr. Jones, nice to see you again.*
>
> What's so good about it?
>
> *Well, it's not pouring rain, and we're moving ahead on your wrongful dismissal action.*
>
> Ya, moving at a snail's pace. Why don't you just get this settled? Any idiot can see the company can't win.
>
> *All right, I can see that you are anxious to get started, so why don't I just ask some questions.*
>
> Ya, whatever.
>
> *Now, you were going to bring in a copy of your last pay stub, showing the severance payment. Do you have that for me today?*
>
> Na, I couldn't find it. I probably threw it out. If you were tough with the damn company, you'd be able to make them do the work and dig that out.
>
> *Yes, we should be able to get that information from the company, but we hoped that, by getting it from you, it would be quicker and save you some money, and I know you have expressed concern about the cost of litigation.*
>
> That's another thing. Why do I have to pay you guys? They're the ones who fired me.
>
> *One of the things we'll be looking for, in either a settlement or a court proceeding, is for the company to pay costs, which would reduce the amount you have to pay.*
>
> Etc., etc.

You get the point. Your client is angry at the company for firing him, and since the company is not at this meeting, he is "dumping" on you. You might be tempted to say to him, "No wonder they fired you, you big jerk." Trust me, this would not be conducive to a good working relationship. The approach to take is not to actually ignore the inappropriate comments but to let them slide by and attempt to redirect the client's energy to more positive endeavours. This can work. However, in this scenario, it is clear that the client almost sees your positive effort as a verbal challenge, prompting him to make another slight or grumpy statement. While it is not a good idea to be confrontational with hostile clients, some ground rules need to be established. Remember, it is not so much whether you can survive this meeting—there will be other dealings with Mr. Jones over the course of the litigation—it's just that a positive working relationship is essential, if you are to obtain the best results for him. I am not a fan of challenging the client at his very first grumpy comment; however, as soon as it is clear that a pattern of hostile behaviour is being established, you should nip it in the bud. Let's see how this might develop, given the earlier scenario.

Good morning, Mr. Jones, nice to see you again.

What's so good about it?

Well, it's not pouring rain, and we're moving ahead on your wrongful dismissal action.

Ya, moving at a snail's pace. Why don't you just get this settled? Any idiot can see the company can't win.

I would suggest a pause right here. Silence has its benefits. First, it gives Mr. Jones a moment or two to think about his behaviour and that it *has consequences* to your relationship. Second, it gives you an opportunity to compose your response. After the pause, you should make sure that you have his full attention—eye contact is essential.

Now, Mr. Jones, I know that you are frustrated by having to take legal action against the company, and you are angry at them for firing you. That is understandable. Anyone in your situation would feel the same way. But, please remember that we are here to help you. In order to help you, in order to achieve the best results we can in the shortest possible time, we need you to work with us—to help us help you. Do you think you can do that for me?

I know it isn't your fault. I'm sorry. I'll do my best to help, where I can.

Few people would insist that they have the right to abuse you. If that does happen, the solution is simple: they can look for other counsel. By dealing with hostile comments directly, you put this issue on the table. Mr. Jones knows he is being childish and petulant. He knows his behaviour is inappropriate, and he is probably aware that it is counterproductive. By stressing that this is a team effort, you have a reasonable chance of getting him on your side, and, particularly, in his circumstances, by having him work with you, he has something positive to do to advance his legal matters toward conclusion. The question at the end is designed to get him to commit to the process; it's like giving his word. Mr. Jones will probably try to behave, with the help of the occasional reminder, if he slips.

Humour, if you are comfortable using it, can be very useful, but it must be something that fits well with your personality if you are going to pull it off. You could respond to the initial grumpy comment with, "My my, someone got up on the wrong side of the bed today." Saying this with a smile and a teasing lilt might work. My wife sees these sorts of people as a personal challenge, and she doesn't let up until they are sharing a laugh with her and their mood is transformed. Personally, I figure anyone is good for one joke, but if a grouch is determined to stay in his foul mood, let him stew in it. (Strangely, most people prefer my wife's company to mine.)

If a client is very hostile, the interview may need to be terminated. You can do this by informing the client that you find it impossible to continue with the interview when faced with his anger. You can ask him if he can set aside his anger and carry on. If it has reached the point where you are feeling physically or emotionally intimidated, you can simply say, "I'm afraid we won't be able to continue today"—and you leave the room. This is not so easy if it is your office, in which case you may wish to call for "back up" before delivering the bad news. Thankfully, such extreme situations are *rare*.

> **"While it is not a good idea to be confrontational with hostile clients, some ground rules need to be established."**

You may find yourself in an interview where a client expresses his frustration inappropriately. He may use abusive or profane language in describing the other party.

Members of a law office are not language police, but certain language is simply not acceptable—it demeans the legal process. It may also upset you personally, or perhaps because the attack is based on gender or race.

Such language is *not* acceptable, and you should tell the client so. "I'm sorry, I find that language inappropriate in this interview and must ask you not to use it." In the case of racial slurs, I inform the client that his language in unacceptable, and I won't tolerate it in the office. Don't be a zealot—you should be willing to tolerate a client slipping and using inappropriate language, particularly when he is upset—but a principled approach is necessary in all dealings with clients. Why would a client expect your firm to be principled in other areas, if not in dealing with the issue of acceptable language?

One thing will probably be consistent: if you ignore the first instance of inappropriate language, you are condoning its use, and the client will—repeatedly and often and more frequently—use this language until you are forced to make a big deal out of it. Nip it in the bud.

Withdrawn Clients

A much more common experience than dealing with hostile clients is dealing with a withdrawn or shy client. Shyness can be either an aspect of personality or a side effect of the situation. It is sometimes difficult to know which, when you are dealing with a new client, but the difference can affect the way you deal with it. If you are not getting sufficient information from your client in response to your questions, there are a few approaches you can try. One is to vary the initial queries and try closed questions instead of open ones. This is often how young children are approached.

> *What is your name?*
>
> Sarah.
>
> *Sarah. That's a beautiful name. And how old are you, Sarah?*
>
> Nine.
>
> *Nine years old? I have a nephew who's nine. His name is Ralph. Where do you live Sarah?*
>
> On 10th Street.

These kind of questions can loosen things up and take some of the anxiety out of the situation. The difficulty—in many circumstances and with children particularly—is that the interviewer doesn't revert to the open questions when the child is warmed up. Important information is being elicited, but the pattern should switch to open questions or a mix of both. But consider the following exchange.

> *Now Sarah, sometimes bad people do things that hurt children. Did your Uncle Bob do bad things to you?*
>
> I guess.
>
> *And did he touch you where he shouldn't?*
>
> Ya.
>
> *And it hurt you when he did these bad things, right?*
>
> Sure.

This questioning has three significant problems. It does a disservice—to the child, the person who is criminally charged, and to the administration of justice. A skillful interviewer would be able to have the child talk about what happened to her without putting words into her mouth. By having the child tell her story, it is possible to discover information that allows the court to weigh the evidence and assess its reliability, because it actually comes from the mouth of the child. Compare the above with the well-known interview that happened between a mother and daughter in the case against a Dr. Khan.

> *Mrs. O:*   *So you were talking to Dr. Khan, were you? What did he say?*
>
> T: He asked me if I wanted a candy. I said, "Yes." And do you know what?
>
> *Mrs. O:*   *What?*
>
> T: He said, "Open your mouth." And do you know what? He put his birdie in my mouth, shook it, and peed in my mouth.

> Mrs. O: *Are you sure?*
>
> T: Yes.
>
> Mrs. O: *You're not lying to me, are you?*
>
> T: No. He put his birdie in my mouth. And he never did give me my candy.

"A skillful interviewer would be able to have the child talk about what happened to her without putting words into her mouth."

This sequence of questions and answers has a ring of truth to it, because what comes from the child are comments in age-appropriate language, from a child who did not appreciate the significance of the event that had occurred. The twist at the end, where the child makes note of the fact that she did not get her candy, is a comment that is credible, in context.

If it is necessary to start a client off with narrow, familiar questions, remember to return to open questions as soon as possible, particularly when dealing with the substance of the interview. When dealing with a client who is giving little response to questions, be patient. Wait. Let the client supplement her own comments. Silence can work wonders.

> *Let's talk about the fight that happened.*
>
> Un huh.
>
> *Tell me how it started.*
>
> I dunno.
>
> *It's important that we have a clear idea of how the fight started in order to help you. Now, please just start at the beginning and say what happened.*
>
> It's just the usual.
>
> [*Pause.*]
>
> You know the way fights usually start.
>
> [*Long pause.*]
>
> Well, Jenny had been teasing me.
>
> *That's good. Tell me more.*
>
> Well, teasing me about being a slut.
>
> [*Pause.*] *Good. Keep going.*
>
> Well, it all started with her so-called boyfriend … .

In conversations, most people can't resist filling in pauses. When you deliberately pause, so that your client expects he should talk, it is doubly difficult for him to remain silent. Remember this is your interview, and you establish the protocol, the expectations. If clients are expected to talk, most will. You are a powerful force in directing how the interview unfolds.

When responding to a minimal answer, a comment like, "Tell me more about that" or "Can you give me more detail on that point?" can also be effective. Letting a client know the importance of thoroughness, perhaps with an example of a situation when thoroughness was essential, may help. In addition, reassuring the client about the confidentiality of the session, that the information that he is providing will remain within the law firm, can help a client who is discussing a sensitive topic.

If you are dealing with a client who simply lacks confidence and is painfully withdrawn, you may need to spend considerably more time in establishing rapport with him. The search for something in common can help, but be aware: it could have a dampening impact if it just reveals that you have nothing in common with the client. If you have any anecdotes that relate to his circumstances, you might employ them, to relax the situation. This is one instance where the usual rule of thumb regarding the proportion of listening time to talking time will be reversed.

Sometimes, a client will "clam up" over a particular topic.

Tell me about the sexual assault.

How did you handle your mother's death?

These are topics that a normally communicative person has difficulty talking about.

The ability of the client to be open about these matters is largely a function of his relationship with the interviewer. A number of factors will increase the likelihood of candor from your client. If he has a good, empathic feeling about you, he will find it much easier to open up.

When dealing with sensitive topics, people often use modified language, even "baby talk." Death becomes "passing on"; sexual intercourse becomes "intimacy" or "family relations." One problem with this is the confusion that may result. I would never have thought that having sex and "family relations" were the same thing. I think of having tea with my parents as family relations, something quite distinct from having sex. If you require honesty from the client, you must give it in return.

Another aspect of language sensitivity emerges when the interviewer appears uncomfortable with the subject. The client will often adopt the same attitude. You do not want your clients avoiding talk about sensitive topics because they think it will make you feel uncomfortable.

Encouragement, patience, silence, and persistence are invaluable tools in drawing out the reluctant client.

> **I** was interviewing a client once, in preparing his will. He had recently been diagnosed with terminal cancer. He was still, to all appearances, healthy and functioning well. In discussing his specific bequests at one point, he commented fondly on a certain possession he had acquired and said it was "to die for." We both looked at each other momentarily and then burst out laughing. He was more comfortable with his death than I was, but he came to me to set his affairs in order before he died, and it would have been a shame if I had approached the whole matter with such discomfort that it made him feel less at ease in going through the process.

"If you require honesty from the client, you must give it in return."

Talkative Clients

Students are often concerned that they will be faced with a talkative client, and that this will absorb so much of their time that they will fall behind in their work. This fear is understandable, especially in a law-firm environment, with all the time-sensitive pressures that exist there, but it tends to be given too much importance in the scheme of things. For example, it is often the rationale put forth for beginning interviews with narrow questions—otherwise the client may go on forever.

Now we have all been victims of the client who talks and talks forever, without ever getting to the point. But these clients are, by far, in the minority, and we should not allow our practice of law to be governed by the exception. The vast majority of clients can summarize their legal concerns, in an initial meeting, in under five minutes. Surely, we can give the client five or even ten minutes of uninterrupted attention. If not, perhaps there is an assembly-line job that needs to be filled.

This said, there will be some clients who need help in getting to the point. This is where your skills come in handy, diplomatically redirecting the client's attention to important details. If he has been going on for some time about the first job that he had out of high school, twenty years ago, it's probably time to become directive.

> *Thank you, Mr. Jones, for that detail, but I need to interrupt to ask you to tell me about the specific concern that brought you here today. We may need to get back to your employment history, but now I want you to focus on the central event, so I can put your comments in context.*

This sort of intervention is usually sufficient to get the client back on track, but if necessary you can intervene again with a comment like, "Your particular approach to housebreaking pets is fascinating, but I am concerned that if we don't get down to the issues, we will be out of time and not be in a position to take any steps on your behalf." It is often helpful to remind the client that time is money and that, by focusing on the important details, he can help you save him money in the long term.

You can structure your questions in a more restrictive manner: "Specifically, in relation to the incident on June 21st, tell me what happened, just on that day." Your client needs to continue feeling appreciated and valued, but you can stress the need to concentrate on the legal issues that need resolution, particularly if they are time-sensitive.

If a particular client has been told before that he is talkative, humour may help get beyond the problem. Whenever a discussion around my house suggests *any* romantic involvement between my wife and me, my 13-year-old son covers his ears, shouting, "Too much information. Too much information!" An interjection like this could bring that client back to the basics in a lighthearted manner.

Another approach is to structure your questions in a very restrictive manner. A series of closed or yes/no questions can cover a lot of ground in a short time period, but remember: by restricting the client so tightly, you can lose important information.

I once worked with a lawyer who was not renowned for his sensitivity. During an interview with a client who rambled on and on, he interrupted them to say, "You're paying me a fortune for every hour I work on your file and—*time is money.*" The lawyer then made a pendulum motion with his finger, saying, "tick-tock, time is money." Whenever the client started to ramble, the lawyer would say, "tick-tock" and wave his finger back and forth. The client would get a panicky look and get right back on track. The lawyer actually reached the point where he just had to wave his finger, without any verbalization, and the client instantly refocused. Obviously, this is not an appropriate way of relating to clients in general, but in a rare instance, it might work. However, a fairly high likelihood exists that a client would take offence to this approach. So, unless you are very confident that it is necessary—and confident that you can "pull it off"—you should use other tactics.

Distressed Clients

Some clients are so emotional—a result of the circumstances they find themselves in—that they simply cannot avoid showing their distress. They may cry throughout the interview or their emotional responses may include mood swings, accompanied by histrionics. Keep in mind that you are there to help this person. A breakdown doesn't have a right or wrong time; it is not a planned approach to dealing with the world; people just get overwhelmed. If you empathize with them and give them permission to have a little cry, that is all most people need. Ignoring the emotion does not make it go away. By acknowledging and accommodating the emotion you can diminish its intensity.

You are not a therapist; don't dabble in this role; but if you do not acknowledge the emotional content, it will repeatedly force its way into the interview, making it difficult or impossible to obtain the information you require to help the client.

You might try this:

> *I'm sorry; perhaps we are going a little too fast. I know that this is a very distressing time for you. There's no rush. Would you like some time alone or can I get you some water?*

Giving space to the client and giving him permission to feel the way he does will usually have a calming influence on a client's emotions. In rare instances, you may have to take a break or continue the interview another time. Let the client know that he has options. Few circumstances mandate immediate action; however, if that is the case, you will need to be a little more directive. If not, you should take some of the pressure off.

> *You seem to be very upset right now; we could take a break or continue another time.*
>
> No, that's OK. I can continue.
>
> *All right. I can appreciate that it may be easier to just continue, now that you are here, but if you do need to break, just let me know.*

It is usually better to continue. Adjourning to another time just means that the client has to live with the problem for that much longer, along with the anxiety of an often-worsening situation where the legal concern is not attended to.

Evasive Clients

Sometimes, clients consciously evade questions or avoid certain avenues of inquiry. When conducting an interview, you need to have your antennae alert to evasion. Most clients do their best to answer your questions, but if your listening skills are keen, you will catch discrepancies. Some involve errors of omission; others are errors of commission.

Errors of omission happen when a client does not purposely mislead but nevertheless allows you to hold the wrong impression. He doesn't correct you on a mistaken assumption. This could even be intentional, essentially a devious effort to mislead. Some clients have developed circuitous methods as their way of dealing with the world. Look for language that shows that the client avoids personal responsibility for his beliefs or behaviour. Attributing feelings or actions to third parties is a method some people use to escape accountability.

People don't like it when they are kept waiting for appointments.

Nobody can figure out how to fill in their tax forms.

Why would anybody want to live like that?

For the client to make a clear statement and to own his thoughts or behaviours, the comments need to be personalized. Try asking, "How do *you* feel about that?" or "What did *you* do in that situation?"—questions that encourage the client to use "I" in his statements.

I hate missing my lunch break.

I never know what to do at railroad crossings.

I don't trust people over 30.

Errors of commission are basically lies. The client tells you something that is not true, which, while a stupid thing to do when interacting with his law firm, is not uncommon. Sometimes, the client tries to help his case by changing the facts, so that he appears more in line with the law. Sometimes, the client just wants you to like him better, to think he is the good guy, because then you will work harder for him. This is a dangerous approach for any client to take, because it will almost certainly result in the lawyer being blindsided.

When listening for evasiveness, focus on whether the client answers your *actual* question. Many people are reluctant to lie in court, but not so reluctant to sidestep a sensitive matter in a conversation or interview.

Were you home at 11 p.m.?

I like to be in bed by 10 each night.

Or,

Did you handle the money from the deposit?

Not really.

You shouldn't accept those kinds of answers. Pursue the client, but try to do so without making him feel threatened. You may need to assure the client about confidentiality before proceeding.

When I asked you if you handled the money from the deposit, you said,
"Not really." It's important that I know whether you handled it in any
way at all. Remember, what you say stays within the law firm. Now,
did you handle the money at any time?

Well, just to count it, but the manager was there the whole time.

Your clients must understand that evasive or even sloppy answers "don't cut it." As a professional interviewer, you set the standards. Your client must perform to those high standards—that is how you obtain excellent results. If the client hadn't been challenged on his "not really" answer, his credibility would have suffered greatly when the manager testified that your client counted the money in his presence.

An interview might go something like this:

Can you describe the fight with your wife?

Well, she went wild and started hitting me with a tennis racket.

Did you touch her in this confrontation?

I never laid a hand on her. (The photographs of his wife show black finger bruises on her upper arms.)

All right. Now, this is very important. I need you to help me with this and to think very carefully. I know these things happened very quickly, and it's easy to overlook something. We have photographs that show your wife with bruises on her upper arms that look like finger marks, from grabbing.

OK. Sure, I grabbed her, to try to stop her from hitting me, but that's all.

Questioning the information from the client does not need to be confrontational. As shown above, the interviewer has stressed the need for the client to think carefully. She has also pointed out the importance of helping her understand all of the evidence relating to this fight. The assurance of confidentiality might also assist, as well as noting, to the client, the significance of the lawyer knowing everything, even allegations that the client feels are unfounded.

Also note, from the passage above, that the client has been provided with a graceful way out. It's not, "You must be lying," but "Help me to understand this evidence," and "I know it's easy to forget these things." Frankly, it *is* easy to forget exactly what happened in the heat of the moment. Many studies have shown that to be true.

Emphasizing that this is a team effort keeps you on the same side as the client. The strategy also allows you to avoid implying he is lying.

Listening for anomalies in the client's version of events is important. Thomas Kuhn, in his book *The Structure of Scientific Revolutions*, describes an anomaly as a red ace of spades in a deck of cards. Flipping through the deck, a person can pass by the card a number of times without stopping, but somewhere in the back of his mind something clicks, telling him that something is wrong. When you, as the interviewer, "see" that red ace, be sure to return to the issue with the client. Sometimes a client uses language in an offhand manner and doesn't even realize he has contradicted himself or information given by other witnesses regarding the events at issue. In the margin of your notepad, remind yourself to question the client about anything that sounds "off" to you. This will help ensure that when the client is later cross-examined, he is well prepared for the questions.

If the lies can't be reconciled and the client remains unrepentant, you may need to point out some facts of life to him. "How do you think a judge would react to what you have said?" or "Imagine what would happen to your evidence if the group of nuns who observed the entire incident testified." Or, "Do you think you may be mistaken about that aspect of the incident, given all the evidence that points in the other direction?" Or simply pointing out the obvious by running through the other evidence already collected.

The point is that some situations will require this direct approach—without being insulting or confrontational. Confrontation may be required, but that should be left to the lawyer to handle, since it may result in the client looking elsewhere for representation, which is not always a bad thing.

A client who hedges what he says should cause you to raise your antennae. Uhm's and aha's, something as simple as a pause before answering a simple question, or the use of fence-straddling responses like, *sort of, mostly, more or less* should send danger signals, calling for further assessment.

Incompetent Clients

As a legal professional, you may be concerned that the client does not have the competence to give instructions. This can happen with aging clients or, otherwise, with people who have just come from a luncheon date with Elvis—I don't mean a client who isn't a competent worker, but one who is not mentally competent. If a client is not competent, your law firm cannot take instructions from him, and there are a number of steps that will need to be taken.

> *Can you tell me a little more about the alien abduction?*

While you may decide to proceed with an interview where you have some concerns about your client's competence, you will need to use the interview as a testing ground, that will provide information to assist the lawyer in making an assessment of competence. You can test a client's memory by asking specific questions that you expect he should be able to answer, to determine if his faculties are in order: name, address, birth date, where and when he was married, how many children he has, things of that sort. Some assessment can be made by taking a fact, say a child's birth date and asking, "How old does that make Sidney?" These sorts of questions can be worked into most interviews, without betraying your concerns about competence.

The ability to translate date of birth to physical age can also be linked to culture and education. I have seen witnesses cite a child's birth date as 72-11-21, but not be able to put an age to that. In instances like this, the witness can be otherwise completely competent, clear, and credible.

With some clients, the concern will not be a significant failure of mental faculties but bizarre mental functioning. Some information and insights about this can be acquired by drawing the client out on certain points.

GENERAL COMMENTS

Aside from the positive impact Valium might have with clients who require more than the usual amount of patience, some tactics are worth restating. Many "difficult" clients require a redirection of their focus. The hostile client needs help in redirecting his anger into avenues that can assist in achieving positive results. The distressed client needs sufficient support so that he can concentrate on providing the information to keep the legal matters on track. The talkative client needs to be focused and refocused, so that he does not spread chaos and confusion in his wake. In your day-to-day interactions, practise redirection in dealing with clients—or even with your family members or acquaintances who lose their focus. By emphasizing the importance of working together to solve the "problem," you can direct the attention and energy—which both of you put into dealing with the situation—in a more productive direction.

Not every unusual story or client necessarily implies incompetence. Some years ago, a compelling, hour-long, television documentary focused on the idea that the United States moon landing was a hoax. You need the context of the Cold War to appreciate the impact of the space race, which sought to upstage the Soviets and calm the mild hysteria prevalent at the time, when otherwise intelligent people believed the Russians were simply trying to get to the moon first so they could sit up there dropping bombs on the rest of us. The point is that you need be sufficiently informed and alert to decide if a client's seemingly bizarre thoughts should be brought to the lawyer's attention.

You are not trained to determine if a client is mentally competent, but when you find yourself in a circumstance where a client makes an incongruous statement, explore the comment: it may relate to an important detail you had overlooked, but it may also point to a mental competence issue that the responsible lawyer should pursue.

CHAPTER QUESTIONS

1. Is it true that paralegal interviewers should only provide legal advice when they are absolutely sure about what they are telling the client?

2. If a client makes an unethical suggestion, you should

   a. tell the client you will get back to them on that, after talking to the lawyer handling the file,

   b. push the silent alarm button and have the firm's goons take the client into the back alley and "deal" with him there,

   c. first determine how much the client is willing to pay for this service, or

   d. politely tell the client that the law firm would not be prepared to consider being involved in what was suggested.

3. How can you deal with a talkative client? How about a withdrawn client?

CHAPTER EXERCISES

Concerning ethical or conflict problems, here are a few scenarios to stretch your mind. How would you react—what would you do—in these circumstances?

1. Your new client, seeking a divorce, calls and says that her husband is going to be calling your office for an appointment. She wants you to tell her husband you can't act for him (which obviously you can't) but she asks that you refer him to lawyer "Z." You ask why that lawyer, and your client says, "He acted for a girlfriend of mine and he's totally incompetent. He's a pushover, afraid to litigate, so my husband will settle for whatever we offer, and that will make your job so much easier."

2. A client asks you to backdate a bill to December of the year before, because it will really help him with his taxes.

3. A client asks if you will have dinner with him.

   a. Does it matter if the client is well-to-do?

   b. Does it matter if the client is married?

4. A client asks if you can keep a secret and then blurts out that he really did commit the sexual assault he is charged with.

5. A client offers you a gift certificate for dinner, if you can put her file to the top of the lawyer's pile.

6. Your client's older brother agrees to pay her bill on condition that he will be directly informed about what is happening at every stage and have input into the planning of strategy.

7. A longstanding client has a purchase that completes today. One document that requires a witness has your client's signature on it but no witness shown. The lawyer has gone fishing, leaving you to finish the filing.

   a. What if the client is also not available?

   b. What if you recognize the client's signature?

   c. What if you can get hold of the client but he can't come to the office before the registry closes?

CHAPTER 9

The Art of Criticism

In Brief

This chapter provides suggestions about how you can take advantage of constructive criticism to improve your interviewing skills. Most people have had negative experiences with critiques. You can become adept at getting and giving criticism. Handling the process, from both positions, requires sensitivity. This is fundamental to the honing of the craft of legal interviewing.

Many of us find criticism hard to take; our egos are more fragile than we like to admit. People who are required by their jobs—or take it upon themselves—to criticize are often fairly "ham-fisted." Lack of training is usually a factor, but critics who anticipate an uncomfortable response may soft-pedal their criticism. Others become aggressive or defensive.

Any act of learning requires feedback. The child who puts a hand on a hot iron receives immediate feedback; pain teaches "do not touch" hot things. As parents, we take these same children and try to teach them to be good by using positive reinforcement. The child says "please" and "thank you" and is praised for the courtesy, sometimes rewarded with candy or some other treat. We should all be happy to receive feedback that will help

Children Learn What They Live

If a child lives with criticism, he learns to condemn.

If a child lives with ridicule, he learns to be shy.

If a child lives with hostility, he learns to fight.

If a child lives with shame, he learns to feel guilty.

If a child lives with tolerance, he learns to be patient.

If a child lives with encouragement, he learns confidence.

If a child lives with praise, he learns appreciation.

If a child lives with fairness, he learns justice.

If a child lives with security, he learns to have faith.

If a child lives with approval, he learns to like himself.

If a child lives with acceptance and friendship, he learns to find love in the world.

—Dorothy Law Nolte (1954)

"To improve at interviewing, two things are vital: practice and criticism."

us change our behaviour so that we improve our performance of a task or improve on how we interact with the world.

To improve our interviewing skills, two things are vital: practice and criticism. One without the other is of little value; it can actually have a negative impact. Experienced lawyers can conduct terrible interviews. Years of practice have only perfected poor technique, so they become consistently bad in conducting every interview. People who don't change may be stubbornly entrenched in their old ways or they may not have any effective feedback mechanisms. Criticism should be accepted in an open manner, and you need to be able to give criticism in a manner that invites the interviewer to listen with an open mind. Barriers to "hearing" criticism are easily erected.

CRITICIZING OTHERS

Criticism that is insightful, sensitive, caring, and focused will be of great assistance in developing your interviewing skills. Criticism that is petty, argumentative, hostile, or irrelevant will not.

Be specific in your critique. Telling an interviewer that she was "really good" gives her nothing to take away and use to improve her skills for future interviews. Far better to tell an interviewer, "I thought it created a good connection between you and the client, when you offered her the box of Kleenex."

The same applies to telling an interviewer that he was "really bad." His ability to hear the criticism will likely become blocked. Try instead to point out the consequences of using a certain tactic.

> *When you pressed the client for details of the fight with his wife, he became defensive and closed off.*

A critic's most important attribute is honesty. Reviewers of theatre, television, film, and literature are often criticized themselves for being predominantly negative. They think either that negative sells or that they can't really be critics unless they find a flaw and tear something down. In interviewing training, criticizing is not about tearing down. At the same time, putting a happy face on and making innocuous nicey-nice comments is of no use whatsoever.

Offering your own perspective, highlighting other ways of approaching a problem, and encouraging the interviewer to expand on some of the more successful aspects of the interview is helpful criticism—and it's non-threatening.

> *Can you think of any terms that describe your client's actions other than "lame brain"?*

> *Did you notice how the client moved away from you when you cut him off the third time?*

> *Have you thought about police interrogation as a career? Just kidding.*

Mean or nasty criticism isn't productive, but there are worse things than bluntness. When students criticize each other, they rarely go too far. Usually, they say it was a "good" interview, even where the quality was barely adequate. Every student will not perform to an excellent standard, but all students can do better with practice linked with honest and effective criticism.

Avoid personalizing the criticism, as in, "You always sound so wimpy" or "Every second word you say is 'aaaa.'" This is not helpful. In the first case, it doesn't give the interviewer anything concrete to work on; in the second case, it's such a blunt instrument that the interviewer probably ends up feeling hurt. It's not *who* does it but *how* they do it, and it should be less about *what* is bad than *how* it could be better.

Take notes in the same way you would during a "real" interview. The critic should have a clear and concise record, so that she can quote the interviewer when discussing different aspects of the session. As the interview begins, the critic should make a note about voice tone and questioning style. It is also very useful to write down the interviewer's questions. The answers can be recorded, but don't lose the interviewer's questions in the shuffle.

After the interview, strike while the iron is hot. The interviewer is much more likely to appreciate the significance of your comments close on the heels of the interview. As memories fade, even your most brilliant comment may be wasted. Giving the interviewer an opportunity to respond to the criticism may be useful; however, this can become an exercise in justification—the interviewer only "digs in," in his own defence, and closes down his receptive channels—in which case it would be better to avoid this approach.

On the other hand, you might be criticized by someone telling you that the client seemed very upset when you pointed out the contradictions in the information he was providing you. In the context of the interview, however, you may have thought that it was important to deal with these contradictions head on, so the client would be aware that you experienced them as obvious without being defensive. Explaining the reasons why you conducted the interview the way you did is part of a learning exchange that is healthy.

> **"As the interview begins, the critic should make a note about voice tone and questioning style."**

Appendix G provides a skeleton outline for students to use in organizing their thoughts when acting as critics. It sketches out *some* areas for comment; however, there are many more—the list is not exhaustive as to what areas may be addressed. Use your listening skills and keep in mind the interviewing principles you have learned. They are the best basis for providing valuable criticism.

Giving positive comments before discussing flaws may help the interviewer hear what you say.

> *I thought you did an excellent job of establishing rapport with the*
> *client. One spot where I thought it broke down was when you told him*
> *to "shut up and listen" to you; otherwise, I felt you made a good*
> *connection.*

The more specific you are, the more helpful your comments will be to the interviewer. If you can offer suggestions of different approaches or language, that is very helpful. And remember, your suggestions are not gospel; they are just suggestions, from your own perspective. What works for you may not fit for someone else.

DASS is one of the best mnemonics for providing constructive feedback. In a book by Patti Hathaway,* DASS stands for Describe, Acknowledge, Specify, and Summarize. Here is how this is designed to work:

1. **D**escribe what you observed.

   When you told the client …

   You struck me as uncomfortable …

2. **A**cknowledge your reaction.

   I was surprised by your language …

   It was an uncomfortable situation …

3. **S**pecify alternatives.

   How about trying …

   Would it have worked better if you …

4. **S**ummarize the benefit.

   By approaching it this way it may help …

   Less stress for the client will help her open up …

Like any other shorthand, the DASS approach may help in some circumstances and not in others.

Only in the rarest of instances will sarcasm or making the interviewer the butt of your joke provide a positive learning experience. That is not to say that adult learners can't share the humour of a faux pas, but try to use a feather to tickle, not a cudgel to brain the interviewer.

Read appendix H carefully to learn more about the value of constructive criticism. With a little introspection, trying different approaches, and a lot of practice, you will discover and develop your own style of interviewing.

One of your tasks as a critic is to keep your ego in check. This process is not about hearing yourself talk and showing how clever you are. It is all about helping the person who is critiqued to improve her interviewing skills. As critic, you can play an important role in that ongoing process.

BEING A CLIENT

An essential part of practising interviewing is learning what it's like to be a client. To do this, the interviewer must take on the role of someone who has need of legal services and is being interviewed. The legal concern you develop for this role-playing should be something you the "client" have experienced in your life—or something someone close to you has experienced. By doing this, the "client" is able to draw upon a fund of knowledge when asked a question that was not anticipated. Having a good imagination is of value as well. If you are playing a scenario and the interviewer asks questions that don't "fit" your script, you will need to fill in the blanks by making up answers. It is best if the interviewer prepares some questions, based

* Patti Hathaway, *Giving and Receiving Feedback: Building Constructive Communication*, rev. ed. (Menlo Park, CA: Crisp Publications, 1998).

on the general area of law, ahead of time, but he should allow for responses that come from the "client," on the spot. And the "client" saying "I don't know" to basic questions is not really an option.

A common mistake made by students acting the role of clients is to *give up* the entire story at the very beginning, in one long monologue. This is not realistic. Although clients usually have a clear idea of what they wish to talk about, they seldom provide *all* of the pertinent data right off the bat. To create a realistic experience, the "client" should leave lots of areas for the interviewer to explore. In role-playing, you need to put yourself in the place of the person whose part you are assuming and respond "in character." Playing an older person while chewing gum and slouching in your chair could be "in character," but other presentations would be more believable. In a student interview I recently observed, the students borrowed a wheelchair from student services to demonstrate a point about accommodating a client's special needs. This touch of realism was very effective and challenged the interviewer to rise to the occasion.

If the interviewer has some real substance to dig for, the challenge will provide him with an opportunity to test his skills, and the session will likely have a much more interesting, realistic feel to it.

BEING CRITICIZED

Listening to criticism is often not easy; the tips of your ears burn, your throat chokes up. But, like a nasty tasting medicine, it's for your own good. Try to let the criticism wash over you. Take it in but let go of the ego part that focuses on the fact that it is about you. Staying detached, if that is possible, will usually help you to understand what is being said and to assess how much of the criticism is valid or helpful. Remember: you are an intelligent, caring, and effective person (or at least you will be by the time you finish this book) and minor missteps, even the fact that you are not a perfect interviewer yet cannot change that fact.

In the end, it is up to you whether you accept or reject criticism. However, a warning goes with this statement: most criticism contains a measure of truth, particularly when the comments come from fellow students who are trying to be helpful.

In responding to feedback, resist taking a stance right away. By committing to a position—whether accepting or rejecting the criticism—you develop an ego investment in your response. By doing that, you create a barrier to changing your perspective. If the assessment is unclear or wishy-washy, perhaps you weren't listening, perhaps the critic didn't make her points clearly enough, or perhaps the critic was unskilled. However, if both you and the critic have treated the session seriously, you should acknowledge each comment, be sure you understand it, and commit yourself to considering it, *really* considering it. If you recognize a grain of truth in the statement, you can acknowledge that as well; there usually is some element of truth behind thoughtful criticism.

I coach a law school client-counselling team. In every competition where my team has been in the final round—as with every other practice or competition round—when they finish competing, we retire to a quiet area to debrief. I offer my criticisms of their performance for their benefit. On three occasions, my team won this competition; they became the international client-counselling champions. But I still had comments about the championship session, to aid them in becoming even better interviewers. Learning the skill of interviewing is an ongoing process, so do not despair of the task or shrink from criticism.

> **"Most criticism contains a measure of truth, particularly when the comments come from fellow students who are trying to be helpful."**

If you do not understand the criticism, don't be afraid to ask for clarification. "When you said my interview stunk, what exactly was it that you felt needed improvement?" If you are feeling a little desperate and unappreciated, you could ask "Was there anything positive in the interview that you feel I could build on?" and seek balance from the negativity. However, most students pussyfoot around criticism, and you are hard-pressed to drag any negatives out of them. You may find yourself begging them "to give it their best shot" in order to make the experience as valuable to you as possible.

Ultimately, what will help you the most is to learn to self-critique. Being able to stand back and look objectively at your performance is a huge step toward teaching yourself interviewing skills. When conducting interviews, don't be shy about asking for feedback from clients. Questions like "How are we doing so far?" or "Are you comfortable with how we are proceeding?" may just elicit polite responses, but these questions may also alert you to areas where your interview has gone off the rails. At the end of each interview, after the client has left, you should take a few moments to evaluate how the interview went and what you could do to improve the process for the next time.

PRACTICE INTERVIEWING

Here are some suggestions about interviews you can conduct to gain experience. The more practice and criticism—from yourself and others—that you acquire, the better you will deal with this task in the workplace.

If possible, videotape your interviews, so you can observe and critique each session later. In each interview, choose a different aspect of interviewing skills development to focus on. Choose from non-verbal communication, different questioning strategies, opening or closing segments, empathic responses, dealing with problem clients, or any other aspects of client interviewing that interest you.

- Interview someone you know about his experience in coming to Canada.

- Interview a friend about her job responsibilities.

- Conduct a role-playing interview with another student. Take the part of a client who has a legal concern such as a motor vehicle accident, breach of contract, landlord/tenant dispute, or some other matter.

- Interview an older person about his early life.

- Interview a child about something important to her.

Taping Interviews

One of the problems in taping real client interviews is that it adds a dimension of awkwardness that is difficult, perhaps impossible, to overcome. However, in learning the craft of interviewing, students should still take advantage of any opportunity to videotape or audiotape practice interviews. These are fairly unobtrusive ways of creating a record that can be reviewed at a later point. It *is* helpful to replay the tape right away, while the interview is fresh in your mind. This helps to refresh your memory about why you took a certain approach or used particular language. Enlist the feedback of the client and any others who are available and willing to give input. It is always helpful if these people are aware of—and committed to—the concept of constructive criticism.

It is also both interesting and valuable to your learning process if you make and review tapes periodically. This allows you to monitor your growth as an interviewer. You will, almost certainly, be pleasantly surprised by the rapid improvement in your interviewing technique. Finally, do not be overly critical. If you focus on every little misstep—each time you say "aaaa" or start to cut a client off—you will become paralyzed, unable to complete an interview. Make a mental note of the aspect you wish to change, promise yourself to work on it, but do not beat yourself up when you slide into old conversational habits. Those patterns die hard. It takes time, practice, and positive criticism to hone these skills.

I often tell students in interviewing classes that, when it comes to criticism, their opinions are as valid as my own. I mean this. Yes, I have a lot more legal experience and interviewing experience than the students, but their life experiences differ from my own. When providing criticism, you innately draw upon your life experiences. Remember, when you are receiving criticism, that the comments come from that other person's perspective on the world.

In teaching a class where we are role-playing interviews, I am struck by the value and diversity of experience that enriches the critiquing process. One mock interview involved a person who had been in an automobile accident. In discussing her injuries, the "client" indicated that, immediately after the accident, both of her thumbs were swollen and sore. The client stated that this injury was caused by the driver's air bag inflating. That comment struck a chord with me, and when the class discussed the interview after, I asked whether anyone else noticed the comment and what line of questioning it might indicate.

One student noted that the fact of the injury confirmed that the accident was significant enough to cause the air bag to inflate. Another student stated that the injury to both thumbs showed that the driver did have both hands on the wheel. Yet another student stated that since the client was a waitress by trade, such an injury would make it impossible to carry trays, etc. Yet another student commented that this type of injury (being in the joint) could result in long-term problems that would not be immediately obvious, such as arthritis.

All of these observations were valid and insightful—and all were different from what I was thinking. What had occurred to me was that such an injury was very painful and, although usually minor, such a sprain could take the client's mind away from other, perhaps more serious, injuries. The client might therefore not mention these injuries initially, in fact may not mention them until the thumb sprains were well on their way to being healed.

Obviously, what had immediately popped into my mind was quite different from what other people thought while watching the same interview. Therefore, the more input you receive from different people with different backgrounds, the greater the potential benefit to you in learning this craft. Naturally, your reaction to the criticism is paramount. Your friends are not likely to volunteer to offer criticism on your practice interviews a second time if, on the first occasion, you tell them that their comments were just "stupid and ignorant."

CHAPTER QUESTIONS

1. Give three adjectives to describe helpful criticism. How about three for unhelpful criticism?

2. In responding to critical feedback, is it important to

    a. immediately justify why you said what you did?

    b. remember how you will "get" that person when it is your turn?

    c. think nice happy thoughts while humming a pleasant tune under your breath? or

    d. try to see the critic's point, from her perspective, and genuinely consider whether there is any validity to it?

CHAPTER EXERCISES

1. List three instances when you received valid criticism.

2. List three instances when you received criticism that was unjustified.

3. Consider how you reacted to each kind of criticism. Could you have dealt with either in a more open or productive manner? Would you change how you reacted, if you had it to do over?

4. Conduct a practice interview with someone you know on a topic of interest to them: his job, a traumatic event, a legal concern, a family problem, an interesting vacation. You should know the general topic area and formulate an objective, as well as a rough "game plan" for the interview. If possible, tape the interview. Afterward, before reviewing the tape, make a few notes about your performance, perhaps choosing to critique one particular aspect of the interview. Ask your "client" to tell you how she experienced the interview, and ask her to share her thoughts about anything she feels could be improved. Insist on honesty; this is a better forum to flub something than in the law office with a real client—although that is not the end of the world, as you will learn. Review the tape carefully. Consider the language used, the non-verbal communication, the questioning style, the rapport—or lack of it—through the use of empathic listening and other factors. Congratulate yourself on being one step closer to excellence in interviewing.

Afterword

Becoming a good interviewer is an evolutionary process. It requires continual practice and criticism. It is not good enough to just do lots of this stuff. To improve, you must evaluate your performance and, whenever possible, have objective input from others. You will soon see dramatic improvement. However, if you are to become that rarest of birds, the excellent interviewer, you must continue to hone your skills. Excellence is well worth pursuing. As with so many other skills, the feeling of accomplishment from having conducted another excellent interview is both gratifying and a confirmation that you have done your part in providing the quality of service that clients have a right to expect from a law firm.

If your interviewing technique slips into a lazy shadow of your former glory, it's usually because of lack of vigilance. Don't become one of those interviewers who says, "I know I should really do this better, but that takes time and energy." Learning to become a good interviewer does take time, but good interviewing saves time in the long run. Most important, for a law office, it avoids errors that could be costly, even devastating, to a client's legal representation. The last word, perhaps the most important word of advice, is to be a professional. You *do* have it in you.

Appendixes

Appendix A Interview Stages and Tasks

Client representation	Purpose	Interviewer's involvement
1. Initial client contact	Make initial contact with the client and develop good rapport with her.	Try to develop a good working relationship with the client early in the process. This can produce better, more-responsive communication with the law firm. She can be kept more informed and thus be more helpful in her legal representation, without distracting the lawyer from his focus. This results in more-efficient and effective representation and less cost to the client, while maintaining a high level of client satisfaction, which is crucial to developing the client base for the firm.
2. Assessment of viability of legal action	In order for a client to make an informed decision about whether to pursue legal action and what form that must take, she needs clear and detailed advice. This advice cannot be given in a vacuum but must be based on detailed knowledge of the facts.	You have a key role in gathering information to assist the lawyer in providing sound legal advice for the client to base her decisions on. Whether the support is in gathering information through interviews with the client or other witnesses to the events or in pursuing other sources of information, the more-complete and thorough the information gathering is, the better position the lawyer is in to advise, and the client is in to make decisions.
3. Negotiation	Negotiation involves putting your best foot forward while maintaining a realistic perspective on the likelihood of success of any particular strategy.	As in the previous category, the lawyer's advice can only be based on the available information about the issues, and the client will make the best decision about pursuing or defending an action based on informed advice. An interviewer who effectively gathers information will increase the client's chances of a successful outcome. While no one can make a really bad case into a really good one, it is remarkable what well-prepared advocacy can do to turn the balance in a client's favour.
4. Trial preparation	They say the best defence is an offence, and being well prepared for trial can provide confidence in negotiation and permit the client to genuinely consider the ultimate step of placing their faith in the court system.	Few people actually wish to proceed to trial, but unless an individual is prepared to proceed to trial, she will be forced to accept a resolution that is less favourable than would be available if she were not ready to go.
5. Trial	The central mission here is to advance the client's position and provide the most favourable interpretation of the facts to assist the client in a successful conclusion from the court.	At this stage, you do whatever it takes to assist the lawyer in dealing with the case on a day-to-day, hour-by-hour basis. In a best-case scenario, the work has all been done, but if something unanticipated happens, you must be prepared to react in a calm and focused manner. This may involve interviewing or re-interviewing witnesses and even helping prepare the client for testifying if there is an unexpected twist in the trial. As long as the client is not under cross-examination, the work of preparation can continue.
6. Post-trial processes	The main goal here is to preserve any gains made by the client and ensure her interests are protected.	While this stage is very important in representing a client, more often than not the lawyer has moved his attention on to more pressing matters. Acting efficiently to advance the client's interests, even at this stage, will prove to be valuable service to the client—and to the law firm.

Appendix B Obstacles to Communication

Obstacle	Junior psychologist's explanation	What to do
Need to be liked.	A client's basic need to be liked can interfere with the information given to the law firm.	We must create an atmosphere where a client feels comfortable in revealing facts that may place him in an unpleasant light.
Boosting chances.	Many clients will selectively screen information because they can imagine a set of facts more favourable to their case than the simple unvarnished truth.	Ensure that the client understands that the only way the law firm can provide effective representation is if it knows all the facts.
Politeness.	A high proportion of people will not correct a lawyer or someone who they feel is "more important" than themselves, even when that person is clearly wrong in what he or she is saying.	Stress the importance of accuracy and teamwork in resolving the dispute.
Avoidance of unpleasantness. (See appendix C for some typical avoidance responses and suggestions for dealing with them.)	Clients may not want to think about past events because they bring back unpleasant memories. They may perceive the role of the lawyer to generate confrontation, which is bound to bring further unpleasant experiences.	Stress the importance of a complete understanding, and underline the role of the law firm to buffer the client from the unpleasant aspects of litigation and to support the client throughout.
Too smart.	Some clients are too smart for their own good. They are constantly trying to be two steps ahead of the interviewer and "reinterpret" the questions based on their (often imperfect) understanding of what you should have asked. Additionally, some too-smart clients simply have an agenda that they are not prepared to share with the law firm.	With clients who are not forthcoming for their own hidden reasons, you must insist on candor. Stress the importance of openness and the cooperative approach to problem solving. If the client will not or can not stop the charade, talk with the lawyer involved. It may not be worth the firm's while to continue with this client.
Not too smart.	Occasionally clients just can't get the point of what the litigation is about. They cannot discern what is relevant and what is irrelevant. Their intellectual "thickness" can be situational, they might otherwise be quite smart people but due to the stress of the legal matters, just not with it. At any rate they are not being helpful in understanding their issue and seeking solutions.	Patience, patience, and more patience. Outline the issues, redirect them to relevant matters, do your best to calm their nerves, and show them that there is an end in sight.

Appendix C   Avoidance Responses

To safeguard against the following avoidance techniques, the interviewer must be faithful to her skills training by asking clear questions, listening to the answers, seeking clarification of ambiguous language, asking mirror questions, and ensuring complete responses to her questions.

Non-answer	Often an over-verbalized, rambling answer that goes all over the map but does not respond to the question that was asked. Evasiveness, but not in a confrontational manner.
Inadequate response	This includes conscious evasiveness, where the client wants the terms defined and looks for other " loopholes" so that the answer can fall between the cracks and she can evade responding but with deniability: "I didn't lie; you just asked the wrong question."
Irrelevant response	This kind of answer is sometimes termed non-responsive. The client answers a question—it just isn't the one you asked. The client appears to be cooperative; she answers; but her response doesn't advance your understanding in any way. This can also happen if the interviewer asks a question in a confusing or jargon-enriched manner.
Half response	Only part of the question is answered. This may be inadvertent, if the interviewer has asked a double-barrelled question. The interviewer has to be alert to the answers and must not be so focused on taking notes or the next question that he doesn't catch that only part of the question has been answered.
Misleading response	The response may purposely mislead or it may be inadvertent, but the client is not taking care to ensure that an accurate picture is being portrayed. Extra attention must be paid to ensure that the meaning is clear beyond question. The misleading client flourishes in grey areas.

Appendix D   Interview Checklist

- ■ Preparation
  - ☐ List of questions (check your list)
  - ☐ Understand the legal issues

- ■ Setting
  - ☐ Comfortable, uninterrupted space for you and the client

- ■ Client rapport
  - ☐ Greeting
  - ☐ Coffee/juice
  - ☐ Introduction/orientation

- ■ Purpose of the interview

  _____

  _____

  _____

  - ☐ Invite the client to outline the circumstances or issues that concern them.
  - ☐ Probe for detail on all aspects of the legal concern.

- ■ Documents/sources of information to obtain from the client
  - ☐ Provide client with follow-up list

  _____

  _____

  _____

- ■ Next steps in the process

  _____

  _____

  _____

Appendix E Inventory of Interviewing Inhibitors

Don't	Do
Judge the client.	Accept the client's statements in a supportive, non-judgmental manner.
Cut off the client.	Let the client tell her story fully; keep track of your questions till after the client has laid it all out for you.
Direct the client, tell her how it's going to be.	Draw the client into the process; get permission for how you wish to proceed.
Argue with the client.	Point out contradictions or inconsistencies and ask for the client's help in understanding what she is telling you.
Ignore client concerns.	Address client concerns when they arise, so they do not fester.
Accept everything the client says unquestioningly.	Be aware of inconsistencies in a client's statements and raise your concerns in a non-threatening manner. These contradictions are usually innocent communication problems, but they don't get better by ignoring them.
Offer solutions. This is not your role or the place to fix on a particular solution.	Check out how the client would like to see the matter ideally resolved. Check out the client's tolerance for a range of solutions.
Minimize client concerns.	Acknowledge client concerns and ensure that they are brought to the lawyer's attention.
Maximize client concerns. Don't whip clients into a frenzy, where the only solution remaining is conquest through litigation.	Provide a calming, rational framework for client concerns. Help clients sort out what is important to them.
Promise.	Refer clients to the lawyer for appraisals of their chances. Assure the client that they are in capable hands and that the firm will do its utmost on her behalf.

Appendix F   Typical Question Starters

Typical open-ended question starters	Typical closed question starters
Tell me about the …	When exactly did …
Describe what happened …	How many …
Outline what went on after …	Can you give me the name …
What happened after …	What date …
Can you explain to me …	Who saw it first?
How would you like to handle …	What colour was …
Give me your reasons for …	How tall was …
Fill me in on the details of …	
Where would you like to start …	
What would you like to see accomplished …	
Why did you …	
Can you add to that?	
Explain to me …	

Appendix G   Critic's Guide to Interview Feedback

Introduction

- ■ Client welcomed
  - ☐ Who's who clear
  - ☐ Procedure clear
- ■ Atmosphere
  - ☐ Physical setting
  - ☐ Emotional setting
- ■ Body language
  - ☐ Eye contact
  - ☐ Verbal tone

Fact Finding

- ■ Client allowed to outline concerns
  - ☐ Attentiveness
  - ☐ Respectfulness/interest shown
  - ☐ Focus maintained

Technique

- ■ Rapport with client
  - ☐ Clarity of language
  - ☐ Pacing
  - ☐ Note taking
  - ☐ Thoroughness

- ■ Questioning styles
  - ☐ Open
  - ☐ Closed
  - ☐ Leading
  - ☐ Yes/no
  - ☐ Either/or
  - ☐ Multiple questions
  - ☐ Probing
    - – Specific probes
    - – Silent probes
  - ☐ Systematic information gathering
- ■ Legal advice avoided
  - ☐ Closing phase
- ■ Summarizes for client
  - ☐ Follow-up plans
  - ☐ Tasks for client
  - ☐ Tasks for interviewer
- ■ Client left with good feeling

Appendix H   Impact of Constructive Criticism

Impact	Rationale
1. Keeps the channels of communication open.	Modifying behavior is a process, not a one-shot effort.
2. Improves rather than weakens self-esteem.	Learners who feel good about themselves feel capable of improving. People with low self-esteem doubt their ability to rise to the challenge.
3. Demonstrates your respect and caring for the other person.	It is easier to accept criticism as valid when you accept that the critic is motivated to help you and not trying to tear you down.
4. Provides specific examples where change would help.	"That really sucked" provides no guidance to improvement. A specific example where improvement is needed is more easily incorporated into a person's behaviour.
5. Breaks the attack/defend pattern, keeping the critic and the recipient on the same side, rather than opposing each other.	Barriers are constructed to defend from the "attack." When a person feels attacked, the walls go up and the perceived attacker ceases to be a source that can be trusted.
6 Harnesses both persons' energy rather than killing the energy in a head-on collision.	You can't make anybody do anything; at best you can temporarily modify behaviour, but if both the critic and the recipient are working together for change, they complement and support each other. A synergistic effect of two quite powerful forces working together is created.
7. Is directed toward clarifying the issues and showing a path to improvement.	The true value of the critic is in her objectivity. Even when we recognize our failings, we often do not see a path to improvement or change. The clarity that can come from others is invaluable in breaking patterns that have been learned, often from childhood.

Appendix I   Interviewing Crossword Puzzle

Across

4. What not to do when the client is talking.
5. Source of notoriously unreliable evidence.
10. Type of questioning where the interviewer interjects in a directive fashion.
12. Question used near the end of an interview to ensure that the client has no other concerns to express or information to provide.
13. Type of client who must be managed with great skill.
14. Putting yourself in another's shoes.
17. Something to try to develop early on in your relationship with the client.
18. Type of listening where you let it wash over you.
21. A non-verbal sign of sadness.
22. Asking many questions all together.
25. Most formal of interviews.
26. Physical location or emotional mood of an interview.
27. Kind of language to use in interviewing, particularly with people who are new to English.
28. Type of interviewee who is not a client.

Down

1. What interviewers should do more than they talk.
2. Have you got what it takes to take it?
3. This differs based on each person's background and experience.
6. Getting all the goods from the client by being _____.
7. When a client avoids the answer, he is being _____.
8. A handy implement for stressful interviews.
9. Necessary for a legal interview to be.
11. Where the law firm cannot act because of other representation.
15. The client gets 100% of yours.
16. What paralegals cannot give clients (two words).
19. Reflecting back to the client what she has said.
20. A way of pursuing information.
23. A question that contains the answer or an assumption not previously stated.
24. Process of starting with broad open questions and progressively narrowing the focus.

Index

dress, style of 121
dyadic (two-way) communication 67

either/or questions 86, 92
emergency witness 10
empathy 21, 75-80, 134
empathic moment 77
errors of commission 134-35
errors of omission 134
ethical challenges 124-26
    confidentiality 125-26
    conflicts of interest 125
expert witness 111, 117
ex parte 70
eye contact 76

facial expressions 76
fact gathering 7, 37, 42, 88, 95, 104, 153
false memory syndrome 97
friendly witness 103
funnel sequence 92-93

gestures 60

hostile witness 103

independent witness 103-4
interpreters 113
interview
    biases of interviewers and clients, effects of
      52-53, 59
    checklist, use of 45, 156
    children 114-18
    clarity 33, 41
    client role-playing, and 144-45, 147
    criticism 47, 141-44, 145-46, 159, 160
    decorum 71
    defined 25
    directive 42, 133
    distractions 52-54
    empowerment 32
    environment 49-50
      emotional 53
      physical 50-52
    inhibitors to 157

non-directive 42
objectives of 27
practice 142, 146-47
preliminary problem identification 42
preparation 28-29, 38
structure 37-38
styles 27, 50
thoroughness 45, 47
types 25
winding down 45-46

leading questions 89-92, 105-6, 110, 114
legal advice 14
legal proceedings
    initial client contact 6-9
    negotiation and trial preparation 9
    trial and post-trial processes 9-10
limitation periods for filing charges 98
listening 63, 78
    active 68-74
    passive 67-68, 69
litigation anxiety 104

mediation 12
memory 107-8
memory aids 96-97
mirroring 74-75
misleading a witness 106
mitigation 29

negotiation 9, 153
non-client witness 99, 103-19
non-verbal communication 59-63, 71
    attentiveness 76
    eye contact 76
    facial expressions 76
    gestures 60
    posture 76
    silence 61, 67, 131
    voice inflection 61-62
note taking 57

open-ended questions 43, 68, 83-86, 118, 130-31, 158

pain diary 99
platitudes 72